A Citizens' I.......

A serious challenge to globalization and the continued destruction of
the environment. In short, there is an alternative.

'The world is no longer divided by the ideologies of "left" and "right",
but by those who accept ecological limits and those who don't.'
Wolfgang Sachs 2003

A Citizens' Income:

A Foundation for
a Sustainable World

Clive Lord

JON CARPENTER
for Clive Lord

Our books may be ordered from bookshops or (post free) from
Jon Carpenter Publishing, Alder House, Market Street, Charlbury,
England OX7 3PH

Please send for our free catalogue

Credit card orders should be phoned or faxed to 01689 870437
or 01608 811969

First published in 2003 for Clive Lord by
Jon Carpenter Publishing
Alder House, Market Street, Charlbury, Oxfordshire OX7 3PH
☎ 01608 811969

ISBN 1 897766 87 4

Printed in England by Antony Rowe Ltd, Eastbourne

Contents

Preface

This book is written for those many people who do not yet share a Green world view, but who do have stirrings of unease that we are not looking after the Planet as well as we ought. It is also written for Green Party supporters as well as others who share similar concerns but who have chosen different paths and strategies

This book makes as few philosophical assumptions as possible. It offers a new insight, albeit at a fairly superficial level, based on the 'Deep Ecology' tenet that we should model society on tribes who live in harmony with their surroundings, but this is confined to one aspect of society. On the other hand it is 'market' oriented only in the sense that since the market *is* dominant, that is where one must start, willy nilly. It is a part of my claim that the ideas in this book may help other norms to emerge. In his book *Rethinking Green Politics* John Barry states (p.160):

> … Although … [Green politics] … may be anti-capitalist, this does not necessarily mean that it is against the institution of the market. The social institution for uncoerced economic exchange can be a part of collective ecological management.

This book assumes that economics will and should remain as part of the ecological decision making process, but that its current dominance must cease.

This is not an academic book, but it has been submitted to academic criticism. I admit frankly that some of the steps in my reasoning are intuitive rather than based on evidence. I further admit that some critics to whom I have submitted this text remain sceptical. In some instances evidence – for or against – my propositions may exist, but mostly they depend on ideas, indeed sea-changes in ideas for which there can be no evidence in advance.

I have resisted suggestions that some sections would benefit from an expansion of the line of argument being pursued on two grounds: the interaction of several different strands which only make sense when considered together is already unavoidably complex, and I am not the best person to do so. I hope and believe that hostile criticism will be balanced by supporters who have the expertise to supply any missing material.

Since writing the first draft of this book, I have read Colin Hines' book *Localization – a Global Manifesto*. I am convinced that these two books should be read in tandem. We share common aims, and the mutual reinforcement will be vital if we are to achieve those aims.

Acknowledgements

I am indebted in varying degrees to all the following people: Lord (Tim) Beaumont, Samuel Brittan, Hazel Dawe, Steve Dawe, Jonathan Dixon, Paul Ekins, Jayne Forbes, Edward Goldsmith, Ian Harkness, Mark Hill, Colin Hines, Lydia Howitt, Jean Lambert, Brian Leslie, Caroline Lucas, Emily McIvor, Alison Marshall, Ed Mayo, Mark Mullany, John Norris, Jonathon Porritt, Dorienne Robinson, Umadevi Sambasian, Cristchi Schmidt, Mike Woodin, Tracy, Marchioness of Worcester, and Michael Yaffey.

Alison Marshall, Umadevi Sambasian and Michael Yaffey in particular helped above and beyond the call of duty.

Although Jenny Jones has not been directly involved in writing this book, if I were to dedicate it to anyone it would be to her, for pushing me into the swimming pool of authorship.

Introduction

This book is an attempt to set down some inter-related ideas which have been buzzing around my head ever since I was shocked out of political apathy in 1972. The *Observer* had just published a summary of *Limits to Growth*, the projection of the then current global economic and industrial trends commissioned by the Club of Rome (a group of industrialists) and carried out by the Massachusetts Institute of Technology (MIT). It came up with the prediction that if those trends continued unchanged, the world as we knew it would hit a pollution and resource shortage crisis in 1995.

It seemed obvious to me that a new political movement would arise in response to this new knowledge, and quickly become a major world force. I resolved to join this new 'conservation' movement as soon as possible. Perhaps an even greater shock to me than the article itself, was the realization in the days and weeks thererafter, that no one else seemed to have noticed this to me seismic new state of affairs. Neither friends, colleagues at work, the media (apart from the original article), nor anyone else with whom I tried to discuss it were the least bit interested in the MIT findings.

I did indeed join the newly-formed PEOPLE (now the Green Party) in March 1973, but by then 'quickly' was obviously over-optimistic. Over the next few months it dawned on me why it might be a long uphill struggle; and yet at the same time I saw reasons why the need for progress might be even more urgent than ever. There have been unexpected, but unsustained 'breakthroughs' of which the 1989 European Election result is probably the best remembered, but there have also been gratuitous reversals which had nothing to do with the difficulties I had expected. Although at the time of writing 30 years later measurable progress has been made, the Green movement still has some way to go before it can claim to be 'a major political force'. The difficulties still confront us, and nothing has diminished the urgency. This book is an attempt to set out these difficulties coherently, and then to offer something which may form a part of the possible answers.

There are substantial practical difficulties. Unlike Die Grünen in Germany for example, which arose from a coalition against specific environmental problems, the British Green Party was founded expressly in response to *Limits*. But once formed, more immediately achievable goals took over. There is a serious tactical conflict between issues to which a still consumerist public can relate immediately, and the more fundamental aims. Furthermore, many who are concerned about ecological issues, whether fundamental or practical, still tend to define their concerns in terms of their previous political loyalties, which hampers cohesive action.

Humankind must sooner or later come to terms with the fact that the Earth is a little ball in space, and the biosphere a thin shell around it. But even if it can be shown that now is the right moment, the problem is not simple. Worrying about abstruse concepts such as climate change is all very well for those who can afford to do so, but millions worldwide have more pressing problems. Who is expected to give a fig for global warming among those who don't know where their next meal is coming from, or who are merely struggling daily to make ends meet? Meanwhile, although the formation of the Club of Rome shows that even multinational capitalists can be ecologically far-sighted, which of them is expected to be the *first* to pull out of the globalization rat race? They are playing poker with the biosphere as the stake, but of more immediate concern to the globalizers is that the first to 'chicken out' will probably be the loser.

But the apologists for business as usual may be right. Perhaps global warming is a false alarm. The Earth has undergone dramatic climate changes in the past, sometimes quite rapidly. Moreover, some of the technology which environmentalists are prone to belittle, and which could never have come about if humans had always stayed in harmony with Nature, may be vital if we are to survive where the dinosaurs did not. The growth oriented outlook developed for perfectly sound reasons, but its momentum remains irresistible. Whenever the right time to switch from growth to sustainability does come, there is no way we could react appropriately as long as expansion remains the dominant orthodoxy.

The exasperating background is that a vacuum has opened up in politics, at least in Britain, and I suspect elsewhere. Apathy dogs all political parties. The electorate deserted the Conservative Party in droves at the 1997 General Election. Disillusion with the Labour government had set in by the time of the European elections in June 1999 to such an extent that only 25% of the electorate voted! The turnout in the 2001 election was, unsurprisingly, at an all time low. If the Green movement can get its political act together, there is a huge opportunity out there waiting to be taken.

I have been advised that I should avoid using the word 'paradigm', or the expression 'paradigm shift', if I hope the general public will read this book. However, as they are central to its purpose, I shall offer definitions here. A paradigm is a world view held by a significant number of people. The beliefs that the Earth is flat, or that it is round, are paradigms, and the change in consensus from one to the other is an example of a paradigm shift. The end of the mediaeval period saw a gradual paradigm shift from a religion-centred view of the world, to the economic and later consumerist and competitive 'neo-liberal' paradigm which holds sway at present in the Western world, and which is still extending its range. Paradigm shifts can however be quite rapid, for example the switch among geologists from believing that the continents were fixed on the surface of the Earth, to realizing that Alfred Wegener's crazy theory was correct – they really are drifting around.

In this book I suggest a novel approach (not a new approach, as I shall explain) to the problems of hardship and insecurity and their relationship to overall wealth. The lack of this approach is hampering the establishment of a viable Green paradigm. Taken in conjunction with the principle of localization, a viable alternative to the apparently irresistible neo-liberal paradigm can emerge. I attempt to answer questions such as how we might cope without relying on economic growth. The expression 'resource productivity has begun to appear in business circles. This is the principle that resources should be used with maximum efficiency in the same way as has always been taken for granted in the case of labour, time or capital. But there is as yet no recognition that this is the only long term justification for growth, or that 'waste productivity' is also necessary. Growth has brought many benefits, but at a price which is often played down. It is now being taken to extremes, and has become dangerous. A paradigm shift is overdue.

— Part One —

First the bad news

I

Space capsule Earth

**Why we should be more careful with the small planet
we live on**

It is probably 3,000 years since the ancient Greeks first noticed that the noonday sun was higher in the sky at Alexandria than it was at Athens. It would not have taken them long to deduce that the Earth was round. In 230 BC Eratosthenes measured the difference – remarkably accurately – so that they even knew how big it was. So far as they were concerned, the Earth was limitless to all intents and purposes. That view, or 'paradigm', has persisted up to the present. Until quite recently, it seemed a perfectly reasonable point of view. Even when all habitable land masses had finally been colonized by Europeans, technological advances continued to offer ever expanding potential. Experience tells us that somebody somewhere will come up with yet another fix for whatever problem confronts us. Humans – still with the mind and body of our stone age ancestors – have adapted surprisingly well to ever more congested conditions, and situations we were never designed to encounter. I think it was Desmond Morris who remarked that the puzzle is not why there are so many murders in New York, but why there are so few. Dimly, at the back of nearly everyone's mind, was the acceptance that there must be limits to physical expansion. Some pessimists believed that there might even be an upper limit on technological innovation. But not yet, not for ages.

The first serious challenge to that view came with the publication of *Limits to Growth* in 1972,[1] and the United Nations Conference on the Human Environment held in Stockholm in the same year. The stunning views of the Earth sent back from space around the same time undoubtedly lent credibility to the possibility of a new paradigm – that the Earth should from now on be thought of as a tiny capsule in space.

One of the factors underlying the MIT study was the exponential principle. Imagine a bottle of fresh milk which contains a single bacterium capable of turning it sour. Suppose it requires 10 billion before you could taste anything amiss, and 100 billion to turn it sour. If the number of bacteria doubles once every hour, it will have a funny taste in just over 33 hours, and go off completely in just over 36. But the crucial aspect is not how soon it happens, but the suddenness of the final crisis. After 30 hours, the milk is still quite fresh, with only 10% of the taste threshold, or 1% of the bacteria which will turn it sour. Of course most aspects of life are much more complex than this simple illustration, with all sorts of checks and balances to alleviate such a crisis. But the bottle of milk shares with the circumstances discussed in this book the fact that it is not a natural occurrence. The important point is that the 'common sense' view that there appears to be plenty of room, or resources, or time, is unduly complacent. This allows those who have a vested interest in prolonging 'business as usual' to postpone effective action until it is too late for coherent, rational solutions.

When economists talk of "3% annual growth in the economy", that means that on average 3% more resources are being used up than in the previous year, and 3% more waste products will need to be accommodated. Furthermore, these levels will be the base line for the next year. To be fair, there are forms of economic growth (i.e. increases in wealth measured in monetary terms) which could *reduce* resource use and pollution, and already do so to a limited extent: recycling industries, organic agriculture, forestry, a switch to renewable energy sources and the use of energy-efficient technologies. Expansion in health services, insurance or banking could also add value with little or no environmental impact. But current methods of measuring economic growth are still quite indiscriminate. Pundits make no distinction between ecologically sound, neutral or damaging innovations. It is of course taken for granted that economic *growth* is essential. Although there are stirrings of sanity, as yet there are few restraints. Responsible and irresponsible developments are all equally welcome provided they add monetary value in the here and now. For example improvements in meat production due to the use of antibiotics which should have been reserved for emergencies count as economic growth. The same goes for hospital and repair work due to more traffic accidents, or corrosion or illness due to air pollution, not to mention the increased sale of cars, or the felling of rainforest.

It is understandable why modern, Western humankind is proud of its achievements, and plays down the drawbacks. But this is based on a short term, anthropocentric world view. In a balanced, complete history of the world, the events of the last 10,000 years, let alone the last 200, have been quite exceptional. The norm is equilibrium, which Gaia, the inter-connected web of life-support systems has always re-established after the many causes of disruption since life first appeared on the Earth. In *A Green History of the World*, Clive Ponting points out that the history of all but pre-agricultural tribes has been a continual leap-frogging of population increase, resource shortages, measures born of desperation which some-times gave a margin to spare, which led in due course to population increase. He says:

> It is difficult to explain why agriculture was adopted. … Agriculture is most definitely not an easier option than gathering and hunting. It requires far more effort in clearing land, sowing, tending and harvesting crops, and in looking after domesticated animals. It does not necessarily provide more nutritious food, nor does it offer greater security because it selects and depends on a far smaller range of land and animals. The one advantage agriculture has over other forms of subsistence is that in return for a greater degree of effort it can provide more food from a smaller area of land. … The expla-nation that best fits modern knowledge is based on increasing population pressure.[2]

The emergence of modern man must have been the result of some fairly extreme evolutionary pressures. It is known that between our closest ape relatives on the one hand and modern, language proficient man lie a whole host of extinct species, who succumbed to the severity of those pressures. Research on mitochondrial DNA now suggests that even humans are all descended from 'Eve' – *one* female who survived 200,000 years ago.[3] Language and large brains must have been vital. Having achieved whatever was necessary to surmount that crisis, 'Adam and Eve' found that it gave them the ability to expand into and colonize adjoining areas. Sooner or later, each human group must have met limits to that colonization, though most would only reach that point after many millennia. The ancestors of the inhabitants of the Brazilian jungle, New Guinea and Australia must have been able to take expansion for granted for almost as long as Europeans and Polynesians.

The reason why agriculture took a long time to spread is now clear in the light of our better understanding of the efficacy of hunter-gathering and 'slash and burn' techniques – *provided the population remains sparse and stable*. But seen in the context of populations spreading into new lands, the puzzle swings back the other way. Inexorably expanding numbers can explain why some groups became so desperate as to practice agriculture, but why and how did most groups instead survive that crisis by returning to Gaian equilibrium? It is only 10,000 years since the first societies failed to limit their populations to the carrying capacity of their environment. The last Ice Age and its aftermath are an obvious cause of the latest disruption, but we need to explore why Gaia has not yet brought the present period of disequilibrium to an end.

Once 'invented', just like the large brain before it, agriculture did more than just solve the problem. It opened up new possibilities. It would however fairly soon lead to an early 'Tragedy of the Commons', which is discussed in the next chapter: the more populous tribes who had found a way of staying out of ecological equilibrium would easily overwhelm any neighbours who did not quickly follow suit. An early development seems to have been some form of hierarchy within society. I would surmise that that is what first closed the door on the principle of sharing basic necessities, which as I intend to establish, is essential for a human group trying to live within its means. From then on, there was always an elite who would see it as being in their interests *not* to share, especially when shortages threatened, as inevitably they must in a society out of ecological balance. So the door back to an ecologically sound way of life was locked. Not until the rise of communism was there a serious attempt to challenge this state of affairs, but this arose in quite the opposite circumstances – as an attempt to share the proceeds of an expanding economy.[4] So the secret which had enabled all pre-agricultural societies to keep their populations within the limits of their environment had been lost. Without it, we are condemned to a continual game of technological and population leapfrog, which clearly cannot go on indefinitely.

In *A Green History of the World* Ponting points out that not only was agriculture anything but a soft option, but it did not even guarantee survival. He refers to Easter Island (discussed in the next chapter), but he points out that at least three other civilizations appear to have collapsed primarily if not entirely due to the over-exploitation of their resource base: the Indus valley and the (separate) Sumerian civilizations(1900 -1800 BC), and the Maya in Central America. The Maya had reached a highly sophisticated level of civilization, building pyramids and with an accurate astronomical based calendar. Research reported in *The Independent* (6th November 2000) has used that fact to reveal that the final collapse of the Maya, with no apparent external threat, was rather more rapid than would be likely if climate change were the cause, taking place between AD 800 and 830. The ruins of the abandoned city of Zimbabwe – in an area now covered in lush vegetation – are also still completely unexplained.

If we are to survive let alone prosper, we must reinstate all essential features of Gaia. In practical terms, that means a stable population, and interacting behaviour by individuals and communities which reinforces the stability, complexity, and diversity of the biosphere. Sustainability and optimum (not necessarily maximum) productivity are the end goals. Whilst at one level the world must function as an organic whole, that most certainly does not entail uniformity, and neither does Gaia depend on centralized control. In Chapter 4 I shall quote evidence that self-regulating systems always develop spontaneously – if the environment is stable.

A vivid illustration of just how far removed are our current economics from Gaia was shown in a recent TV documentary on rainforest destruction. It showed a felled 40 metre brazil nut tree, on land being converted to cattle ranching. The commentary explained that the food produced by the tree left upright would have exceeded the expected production of the land it now covered. The tree's production had of course been long term. The ranch would be lucky to last five years. Or take the Nile valley, which supported agriculture continuously for 7,000 years. The silt which annually fertilized the entire length is now simply piling up behind the Aswan High Dam. Egypt is now almost totally dependent on imported artificial fertilizers.

Gaia, or Nature if you prefer, has ways of punishing disobedience, as the remains of lost civilizations testify. She employs the horsemen of the Apocalypse – war, famine and disease, as necessary. Even in routine situations Nature can be quite cruel, for example where chicks kill their siblings if the food supply is scarce. A prey species may 'need' predators to keep them from over-grazing, but their life is one of permanent fear and the loss of their young. Many of the tribes which did achieve ecological equilibrium probably practised infanticide. The lesson for modern humans is that we can choose our own methods, but we must obey all Nature's rules.

But there is a puzzle. The Tragedy of the Commons is a real threat, and it has undoubtedly been taken to its grisly conclusion more than once, yet it is far from being the norm. In Chapter 2 I discuss its potential for instability, but why does it not break out routinely? There is a very simple answer: it is a 'default setting' which will end any period of expansion when it reaches its limits if nothing better intervenes. Two aspects can be identified: it only seems to occur where the environment has been destabilized, and it involves competition escaping beyond its normal boundaries. In homeostatic situations competition plays a role, but only within clearly defined limits, subordinate to the overall regulatory mechanisms.[5] We lack information on how Gaia effects a return to homeostasis after environmental disruption.

But some human tribes have successfully outwitted Gaia for up to ten millennia, and have evolved a formidable philosophy to match. Not to worry, say the conventional pundits. Business is extremely resourceful. For example, the fourfold oil price rise in 1973 led to much more careful use of oil world-wide. There is now a flourishing waste disposal industry. (This in itself is no bad thing. It will be a vital component of a truly Green society, once some coherent rules for sustainability are in place.) The hour in the 'milk-bottle' example (i.e the period over which the activity in question doubles) represents 20 or more years at relatively buoyant levels of economic growth. So to carry the 'milk going sour' analogy a little further, if after several centuries of economic growth we start getting warning signs that we are approaching the limits of the Earth's ability to cope, we may have several decades to find more technological fixes to postpone the deadline still further.

The foregoing assumes that warning signs will appear – and be heeded – well before saturation point. There is a case study illustrating in microcosm the danger of a false sense of security leading to a sudden resource crisis: the collapse of the fishing industry off the east coast of North America in the early 1990s. To quote Dick Russell, a freelance writer living in Boston, Massachusetts:

> Canada's Grand Banks and New England's Georges Banks – once among the most plentiful fishing grounds anywhere – have undergone complete collapse. With the virtual disappearance of haddock, cod and yellowtail flounder, an emergency federal closure of more than 6000 square miles off the Massachusetts coast was ordered in late 1994, shutting down a $200-million-a-year industry.[6]

Or Elisabeth Brubaker:

> Five centuries ago, the area now known as Canada's Atlantic coast offered some of the world's best fishing. After John Cabot's voyage to Newfoundland in 1497, the crew returned to England with tales of a sea "swarming with fish, which could be taken not only with the net but in baskets let down with a stone, so that it sinks in the water."… throughout the following centuries, fishermen sailed from Portugal, France, Spain, and England to catch between 100,000 and

200,000 tonnes of cod a year. The ocean remained bountiful. All assumed boundless cod stocks. And given the fleets' technological limitations, they probably were. In 1885, the Canadian Ministry of Agriculture predicted, "Unless the order of nature is overthrown, for centuries to come our fisheries will continue to be fertile."

The overthrow took less than a century... Cod catches tripled from an annual average of 500,000 tonnes in the first half of this century to 1,475,000 tonnes in 1968. In the 15 years between 1960 and 1975, the 200 factory trawlers plying the waters off Newfoundland took as many northern cod as had been caught in the 250 years following Cabot's arrival in Newfoundland.

The glory days would soon end. By 1978, cod catches were just 404,000 tonnes. Many hoped that Canada's establishment of a 200-nautical-mile Exclusive Economic Zone would allow stocks to recover. But chasing foreign boats from Canadian waters did little for the stocks, since Canadian boats soon took their places. After a brief recovery in the 1980s, cod catches plummeted, falling from 508,000 tonnes in 1982, to 475,000 tonnes in 1986, to 461,000 tonnes in 1988, to 384,000 tonnes in 1990, and to 183,000 tonnes in 1992. In 1996, four years after the first moratorium, fishermen caught only 13,000 tonnes of cod.[7]

'Vested interests' need not invariably mean big business. They include ordinary people who have simply made their living in the same way for generations.

There is a body of opinion, to which I belong, which takes the view that a new paradigm is needed now.[8] Even if the end of the world as we know it is not at hand, a new ecological way of looking at the world will take time to develop and to establish itself in the minds of large numbers of people. Unfortunately the early proponents of the new paradigm were mostly scientists who made unduly pessimistic predictions which have not so far been substantiated. Paul Ehrlich made doom laden prophecies on population[9] and commodity prices[10] which did not materialize. *Limits to Growth* has not exactly been falsified, as there have been a number of factors including recessions in industrial and economic activity which would extend the timescale. The sudden fourfold increase in the price of crude oil in 1973 was not seen as an early symptom of the *Limits* scenario, but it did kick-start a limited, but continuous process of seeking energy efficiency and reducing the use of physical resources in manufacturing. However, *Limits* did correctly predict that pollution problems would be a limiting factor before resource exhaustion, but it has a simplistic look about it now. Environmentalists today have a view of Gaia as an inter-connected web of life-support systems that is much more sophisticated than the earlier scenario of crude resource exhaustion or pollution.

The alleged failures on the part of scientists to correctly forecast the precise course or timing of the end of economic growth have been compounded by the splintered response from those of us who have tried to take these warnings seriously. I shall argue that independent Green parties are vital, but far more people have chosen to support various other parties or pressure groups (a necessary component), or to take direct action. This last is often heroic and headline-grabbing (also vital) but it neither obstructs the march of misguided progress for long, nor provides a joined-up political programme which is necessary if environmental protection is ever to become a priority. As a result, those who have vested interests, or who merely believe we are not yet in danger, have easily rubbished our efforts, despite the predictions which *are* coming true.

There has been some progress. At the Earth Summit on climate change held in Rio de Janeiro in 1992, the UK and other developed countries agreed a voluntary target of returning their emissions of carbon dioxide and other greenhouse gases to 1990 levels by 2000 under the Framework Convention on Climate Change. At Kyoto in December 1997 the 174 parties to the Convention drew up a new Protocol. This would reduce developed country emissions of a basket of the six principal man-made greenhouse gases overall to 5.2% below 1990 levels over the period 2008-2012. In contrast to 1992, this target was intended to be a legally binding commitment. In June 1998 at a meeting of the European Environment Ministers, the UK took on a reduction target of 12.5%. The Department of the Environment, Transport and the Regions (DETR) published a Consultation Paper in October 1998, on how to achieve this.[11] The Paper went further, and stated as its aim "to start a national debate on how we can move beyond our legally binding target towards a 20% reduction in CO_2 emissions". Other countries in the EU have even higher national targets. The Paper set a target of 10% of the UK's energy needs from renewable sources by 2010. It also stated that the June 1998 Environment Council set EU wide targets for energy efficiency.

Climate change is now recognized in some quarters, but the will to implement all or any of these measures is clearly still missing. At the first sign of opposition from a sectional interest a climb down seems to be the general response. Britain brought in the annual 'fuel tax escalator', which was supposed to be a contribution to these legally binding and voluntary targets. The Chancellor of the Exchequer had discontinued the escalator even before the oil refinery blockades in September 2000. In November 2000 the conference in The Hague intended to finalize the 'binding' Kyoto agreement failed to do so. Six months later, the newly elected George W. Bush reneged on the existing US commitment to the Kyoto Protocol. All this is against the background of official scientific advice by the Inter-governmental Panel on Climate Change (IPCC) that cuts in emissions of 60-80% in CO_2 emissions are needed.[12]

Meanwhile unprecedented violent weather in Honduras, Orissa and Venezuela during 1999, and even across central Europe, accompanies consecutive annual record high global temperatures. In February 2000 Mozambique was devastated by the worst cyclone for 50 years. The town of Malton in North Yorkshire was flooded twice within two years in 1998 and 2000 to a depth greater than ever before recorded. Perhaps all these scenes on our television screens can still be dismissed as exceptional, statistical freaks. But a particularly ominous event appears to have wreaked no destruction on human lives or property, so it received no such coverage – only a small report in the *Independent* on 4th February 2000.[13]

> Two days of apocalyptic rain… where it normally drizzles for half an hour every two years, have damaged the Nazca Lines 250 miles south east of Lima, in Peru. These have survived intact since they were made between 1,100 and 2,300 years ago. … Flash floods near the area two years ago were shrugged off as an aberration. But this time at least six of the 16 distinctive patterns are noticeably smudged.

The scientific warnings were that the first sign of significant global warming would not be that we would feel warmer, but that we should expect progressively more violence in weather patterns The 1980s and 1990s have each been the warmest decade since world-wide records began. The IPCC was set up by the United Nations in the late 1980s in response to growing scientific and public alarm, and its reports indicate that the consequences of global warming on the scale which it predicts will be profound for the whole of the world. Not only will global temperatures be higher than at any time during the last 100,000 years, but the speed with which these will be reached will be unprecedented.[12]

However I do not intend to dwell on the arguments in favour of a sustainable society. The case for that has been made already by others much better qualified than I am. I propose to stand on their shoulders. My starting point is the precautionary principle: the rule that when assessing the pros and cons of any proposed innovation where the dangers cannot be reliably estimated, we should err on the side of not introducing it.

Even if the need for a 'space capsule' consensus world-wide is not as urgent as some of us fear, now would still be a prudent time to start thinking along those lines, to make sure the world has a safety margin. Until that consensus is expressed in coherent political action, again world-wide, we run the risk that the present tendency of 'too little, too late' in the face of short term interests will persist, leading to more and bigger 'Grand Banks' type crises, and a continued reluctance to accept the possible consequences of climate deterioration.

There are eloquent apologists who claim that humans need not yet, if ever obey Gaia's rules,[14] but the dynamics of the dominant world culture are such that it could not – cannot – respond to warning signs whenever they do become unmistakable. I believe that only political parties whose core principles are based on the space capsule paradigm, in other words, Green Parties, can achieve what is needed, but first I must explore a major obstacle to an ecological world-view before suggesting a possible part of the answer.

Notes and References

1   Meadows, Donella and Dennis (1972), *Limits to Growth*, Earth Island, London.

2   Ponting, Clive (1991), *A Green History of the World*, Sinclair Stevenson, London, pp41-42.

3   Cann, Rebecca L., Stoneking, Mark, and Wilson, Allan C., 'Mitochondrial DNA and Human Evolution,' *Nature,* 325 (1987), pp31-36.

4   Communism was arguably not egalitarian in practice, but it was the first regime which even paid lip service to the notion of equality.

5   See Hines, Colin (2000), *Localization – a Global Manifesto*, Earthscan, London, Chapter 9 for a discussion of the role of competition in a sustainable society.

6   Russell, Dick, freelance writer, Boston Mass Internet posting.

7   Brubaker, Elisabeth, *Cod don't vote How politics destroyed Atlantic Canada's fisheries.* An Internet discussion. Email ElisabethBrubaker@nextcity.com or PerspectiveCDV@nextcity.com

8   For a comprehensive account of an ecological world-view, see Goldsmith, Edward (1996), *The Way*, Themis Books, Dartington,

Chapters 52 onward. Shorter, and easier to read introductions to a Green world view include Beaumont, Tim (1997), *The End of the Yellow Brick Road*, Jon Carpenter Publishing, Oxford, or Lambert, Jean (1996) *No Change? No Chance!*, Jon Carpenter Publishing. In this context, see also Hines, Colin (2000) *Localization – A Global Manifesto*, Earthscan, London.

9   Ehrlich, Paul (1972), *Population/Resources/Environment*, Freeman, San Francisco.

10 In 1980, economist Julian Simon and biologist Paul Ehrlich decided to put their money where their predictions were. Ehrlich had been predicting massive shortages in various natural resources for decades, while Simon claimed natural resources were infinite. Simon offered Ehrlich a bet centered on the market price of metals. Ehrlich would pick a quantity of any five metals he liked worth $1,000 in 1980. If the 1990 value of the metals, after adjusting for inflation, was more than $1,000 (i.e. the metals became more scarce), Ehrlich would win. If, however, the value of the metals after inflation was less than $1,000 (i.e. the metals became less scarce), Simon would win. The loser would mail the winner a check for the change in price. Ehrlich agreed to the bet and chose copper, chrome, nickel, tin and tungsten. By 1990, all five metals were below their real price level in 1970. Ehrlich lost the bet and sent Simon a check for $576.07. Prices of the metals chosen fell so much that Simon would have won the bet even if the prices hadn't been adjusted for inflation (Bast 1994, p.124).
Quoted from Brian Cornell "Julian Simon's bet with Paul Ehrlich" Overpopulation.com. Found on the Internet.

11 Department of Trade Industry & the Regions (DETR) Website

12 Intergovernmental Panel on Climate Change (IPCC) *First Assessment Report* (1990), *Second Assessment Report* (1995/96), *Third Assessment Report* (2001), Cambridge University Press.

13 *The Independent* 4th February 2000.

14 For example Lomborg, Bjørn (2001), *The Skeptical Environmentalist*, Cambridge University Press.

II

The Tragedy of the Commons

A serious obstacle to doing what is necessary

'The Tragedy of the Commons' was the title of an essay published by Garrett Hardin in 1968.[1] I first read it in *Towards a Steady State Economy*, edited by Herman Daly (1973). It made a profound impression on me at a time when I was new to environmental politics, and my whole view of life (my 'paradigm') was in the melting-pot.

Hardin starts by asserting that there is a class of problems to which there is no technical solution. He uses the example of what he, an American, calls 'tick-tack-toe', and in Britain we call noughts and crosses. If neither player makes a mistake, then no one can win. (Some may remember this being used to dramatic effect in the film *Dr Strangelove*.) He then argues that world population and pollution are problems in this class. Technology can take us so far, but ultimately a finite world can only support a finite population, or absorb a finite amount of waste matter. Sooner or later we must make choices between maximum and optimum, having given those terms meaningful definitions. Remember, Hardin was writing in 1968, four years before the beginning of the sea-change made possible by *Limits to Growth*, and at a time when there was utter confidence in technology to solve all or any problems.

Hardin then quotes a pamphlet published in 1833 by an amateur mathematician named William Foster Lloyd, *Two Lectures on the Checks to Population*, to explain what he calls 'the tragedy of freedom in a commons'. Hardin uses the term 'Tragedy' in the sense of Greek tragedy – not unhappiness per se, but the remorselessness of a given chain of events, and the futility of trying to escape it. He explains:

> The tragedy of the commons develops in this way. Picture a pasture open to all. It is to be expected that each herdsman will try to keep

as many cattle as possible on the commons. Such an arrangement may work reasonably satisfactorily for centuries because tribal wars, poaching, and disease keep the numbers of both man and beast well below the carrying capacity of the land. Finally, however, comes the day of reckoning, that is, the day when the long-desired goal of social stability becomes a reality. At this point, the inherent logic of the commons remorselessly generates tragedy.

As a rational being, each herdsman seeks to maximize his gain. Explicitly or implicitly, more or less consciously, he asks, "What is the utility *to me* of adding one more animal to my herd?" This utility has one negative and one positive component.

1. The positive component is a function of the increment of one animal. Since the herdsman receives all the proceeds from the sale of the additional animal, the positive utility is nearly + 1.

2. The negative component is a function of the additional over-grazing created by one more animal. Since, however, the effects of overgrazing are shared by all the herdsmen, the negative utility for any particular decision–making herdsman is only a fraction of − 1.

Adding together the component partial utilities, the rational herdsman concludes that the only sensible course for him to pursue is to add another animal to his herd. And another... But this is the conclusion reached by each and every rational herdsman sharing a commons. Therein is the tragedy. Each man is locked into a system that compels him to increase his herd without limit — in a world that is limited. Ruin is the destination toward which all men rush, each pursuing his own best interest in a society that believes in the freedom of the commons. Freedom in a commons brings ruin to all.

After discussing the limitations of some apparently easier or more obvious answers, the solution which Hardin proposes is 'mutual coercion mutually agreed upon'. He cites taxation as an existing example of this, and uses parking charges backed up by fines as an illustration of how access to a commons can be regulated. So far so good. Unfortunately that is as far as Hardin's essay takes matters. He does not deal with the formi-dable difficulties on the way to agreeing effective mutual coercion world-wide over the vast range of topics where the Tragedy of the Commons is already a serious problem. In fairness, many examples of his thesis have emerged since he wrote it, notably the whole phenomenon of globalization. Examples now include the breakdown in the course of

2000-2001 of the 1997 Kyoto Protocol quoted earlier, and the limited effectiveness of the 2002 Johannesburg Earth Summit.

In order to explore these difficulties I propose to start from the situation outlined in the parable just quoted. I shall call this 'Scenario One'. Each herdsman with access to the commons will approach the situation differently. One, let us call him Alfred, fears over-grazing sooner than all the others. They smile, and tell him that if he wishes to solve the problem that exists only in his mind by reducing his herd, no one will stop him. If he does so, he will have the least power to influence events when the crunch really does arrive. But the parable assumes that everyone is acting rationally. Alfred swallows his misgivings and carries on as before.

In due course more and more herdsmen recognize that although Alfred was unduly pessimistic to begin with, the time is approaching when he may have a point. So long as they are in a minority nothing changes, but eventually most of the herdsmen accept that they will have to do something. Rational – i.e. rationing – solutions are proposed, but a significant minority, led by the ebullient Bernard, will have none of it. They have centuries of common sense on their side. They do not accept that over-grazing is going to happen. Not yet at any rate. The problem may be solved in the ways it always has been. Besides, there are all sorts of new strains of grass being developed. They could chop down more forest and extend the common pasture, or perhaps they could even...

At this point, coercion could be brought to bear by the majority on themselves as well as the objectors. Remember, everyone is assumed to be acting rationally according to the situation as they see it. It would not be a happy ending, because it is unlikely to be peaceful. It is not too fanciful to guess that the Alfreds of this hypothetical world are by nature quiet, self-effacing types, and the Bernards are more aggressive and accustomed to being tactically astute in their dealings in the cattle market. Even an overwhelming nominal majority may not be enough. Above all, it would certainly not be mutual or agreed upon.

Another scenario could be that some herdsmen do exercise restraint.[2] But if they do, Bernard and his friends will grow relatively richer and more powerful, so that when the crisis does break, it is the worst offenders who are in control. No, we are dealing with a rational community. No one will allow that to happen to themselves as individuals. Either everyone is subject to enforceable restraints, or everyone carries on headlong into Tragedy. This is 'Scenario Two'.

A variation which cannot be ruled out is that Bernard is not being entirely honest. His aggressive manner has worked well enough in the past, and at the back of his mind is the determination that if things do go wrong, he will make sure that he is in a position of strength, so that he is not the loser. On a sinking ship, there are often A, who will risk their life for others, and B, who will climb over heads to reach the last place in the lifeboat.

Wait a minute! I just referred to 'a rational community'. The parable mentions no community, only herdsmen. For all we know they come from far and wide. I have implied, with no justification, that all the characters in this 'Tragedy' do at least meet and talk. Even if we assume that they all know of each others existence, as do nation states in the real world, not until all conceivable users of the common pasture are fully involved in a real community can we be sure of either effective coercion or mutual agreement. Until that happens, Scenario Two proceeds apace.

Unfortunately this is no parable. It may have seemed theoretical when it was first written, but it is happening in reality. The pasture is the biosphere – the thin shell within which life is possible which surrounds a ball only 8,000 miles (13,000 Km.) in diameter. The community must include everyone, and every nation on Earth. The collapse of the Grand Banks fisheries off Newfoundland followed almost exactly this course. Scientists' warnings to the local fishermen had gone unheeded for years, but it was boats from Spain that precipitated the final swift destruction of what had been a truly enormous resource.[3] Two decades earlier, the same Tragedy was enacted at the expense of the blue whale – the largest animal that has ever lived on Earth. Despite these precedents, the same play is currently being performed on the European side of the North Atlantic. It probably has some of the same actors.

In case anyone doubts the determination and ruthlessness of the real life 'Bernards', let me quote again from Elizabeth Brubaker, on the collapse of Newfoundland fishing stocks:[4]

The fact that this ecological and economic disaster could have been avoided makes it even more tragic. For too much of the history of the Atlantic fisheries, the wrong people have been making the wrong decisions for the wrong reasons. Politicians have permitted catch levels far beyond those recommended by their own scientists. They have subsidized expansion of the fishery despite countless warnings of overcapacity. Like political piranhas, they have cleaned out the fisheries in their greed to snatch the next election; this species of leader leaves nothing behind to sustain those who will soon follow.

Canada's fisheries managers tried desperately to blame the

groundfish collapse on forces beyond their control. Colder water temperatures, they suggested, had driven the cod away, while an exploding seal population had eaten both the cod and the capelin, the cod's favorite food. In fact, such environmental factors played minor roles. The real problem, scientists now widely agree, was that the politicians and bureaucrats in charge not only permitted but actually encouraged overfishing.

Before I discuss the global implications of the Tragedy, I wish to illustrate the problem of Scenario Two with local examples. I live in Batley, a small town at the geographical centre of the West Yorkshire conurbation. There are five local authorities, Leeds, Bradford Wakefield, Calderdale, and Kirklees. Calderdale consists of Halifax and several smaller towns, and Kirklees is based on Huddersfield, but includes Batley among other towns. Altogether some two million people live and work in a huge ring around us, but until recently Batley included large tracts of unspoilt green land. It still does, but because of its central position, and also being close to the M62 motorway, it is under severe pressure to be developed for housing, retail outlets and light industry. The green areas are disappearing quite rapidly.

There is growing opposition among residents, but the most they can hope for is to delay specific proposals. Mostly they go through anyway. Kirklees has recently completed its 10-year development plan, which allocates huge swathes of Batley for development of one kind or another, so that applications which would have been resisted now have a much easier passage. The argument is of course that the prosperity of Kirklees depends on development. The unspoken component of the pressure is "If Kirklees does not snap up this once-and-for-all opportunity, Leeds/Bradford/Wakefield/Calderdale or perhaps even some other authority will."

Over the last three decades Batley has developed as a centre of the bedding industry. One such firm wished to expand from its nineteenth Century factory to a greenfield site which was more vigorously defended by local residents than most. The firm threatened Kirklees Council that if they did not get the site, they would re-locate to another part of the country, where they had connections. They got their site. I personally think they were bluffing. They would have lost the advantage of factors which cause an industry to concentrate in one locality, and I suspect that the area they mentioned was subject to much the same pressures as West Yorkshire. But I for one would not have dared to call their bluff. Like

Alfred, I am a rational man. The other area might also have overridden local residents to snap up such a gift. It is cases like this which epitomize the conflict between economic expansion and the environment as we approach the limits of the environment to cope.

A much larger area met with far less opposition because there were no residents in the immediate vicinity. It now comprises a huge industrial estate and retail park, including IKEA and several other national and international concerns, an extensive entertainment complex, of which Showcase Cinemas is the nucleus, and a whole range of national brand eating places. Due to its appearance – the area is elevated and visible for miles – it has been dubbed 'Las Vegas'.

Had I had the courage of my convictions, I would have voiced opposition to this as to all the other encroachments. All the usual environmental objections applied. It would take (and has taken) life from the town and city centres nearby. It shifts trade from small, locally based businesses to transnationals. It is on a bus route, but the buses do not run at times suited to entertainment, and access is almost exclusively by car. It is just the kind of indiscriminate conventional economic growth which cannot go on unchecked if we are to be serious about 'Space Capsule Earth'. All this was quite apart from the loss of farmland which had lain derelict for several years in anticipation of the forthcoming bonanza.

Very few people live within walking distance, so there was little or no public concern. I kept quiet on this occasion, and it is just as well that I did. The whole complex is a rip-roaring success. Its patrons obviously think so: all the car parks are full. Anyone who has invested in it must be very pleased. Like the bedding factory, how could I have justified all this very real prosperity in conventional terms being thrown away by Kirklees, and going to Leeds/Bradford/Wakefield/Calderdale or some other authority? Meanwhile none of Kirklees' competitors are sitting on their hands. This pattern is repeated endlessly the length and breadth of the country in huge trading estates: Gateshead Metro Centre, Brent Cross, Meadowhall (Sheffield), and many more. Scenario Two is alive and well, and living in West Yorkshire and beyond.

The principle underlying Scenario Two applies to all kinds of situations. Services such as the Police, education and health are all being starved of public funds in the name of global competitiveness. It is why limitations on arms sales to unpleasant regimes are difficult to pin down. "If we don't, somebody less scrupulous will." There is no doubting the loss of prosperity when the tank factory in East Leeds closed. Which car manufacturer is expected to be the first to reduce production on the grounds of climate change? The same argument applies across the whole range of consumer durables. Such battles have already been fought, for example in the steel and shipbuilding industries. But that is the point. They have been decided by conflict with winners and losers, not by mutual agreement in advance of a crisis which was clearly looming.

Scenario Two made a dramatic entrance in Europe in September 2000 in the shape of fuel blockades which swept through most countries in the European Union. First France, and then Britain was paralysed by farmers, fishermen and road hauliers blockading oil refineries. Britain was cited as the country with the highest fuel prices, (strictly true only in comparison with France and Germany), but this ignores contrary factors such as the absence of road tolls and the comparatively inefficient rail network. The blockades were effective because the apparent victims and even the public at large supported them wholeheartedly,[5] despite the inconvenience and indeed sheer panic. There were distinct echoes of the events leading up to the Grand Banks fisheries disaster. There was a brilliant cartoon in the *Independent* newspaper, of a Third World flood victim marooned in a dead tree holding up a placard which said, "The price of petrol is too high". But that did not stop me 'panic buying' petrol when I had the opportunity, along with all the other car drivers. Once again collective insanity resulted from each of us acting rationally in pursuance of our short-term individual interests.

The same forces are at work over the question of housing on greenfield sites, but here another factor could be involved, to which I shall have to return later: population pressure. Population increase in Britain is of course quite small, and localized in its effect. On the face of it, population is the least of a whole range of pressures driving the housing market. But in some areas resistance is increasing to encroachments of any kind – evidence that we may be approaching a perceived saturation point. Volatile house prices are due to other causes, but population pressure will not help. In a room which will comfortably hold 100 people, as long as there are say 98 or fewer, one leaving or entering will not be noticed. But over 100 each extra person – or for that matter any other normally insignificant added pressure, will create discomfort out of all proportion for everyone. This is just another aspect of Garrett Hardin's concept of the 'carrying capacity' of a commons.

But it is the global examples of the working of the Tragedy of the Commons which are of the greatest concern: those whose effects ignore national boundaries. Commercial considerations dominate environmental ones in the nuclear power and waste reprocessing industries. Genetically modified crops have the potential to affect the environment worldwide in unpredictable and irreversible ways. Yet just as in Garrett Hardin's parable, the benefit to the GM manufacturers is +1, and they estimate the harm to themselves as only a fraction of -1. This has been compounded in Britain by government support for GM crops. Its reasoning was quite understandable. If there are immense profits to be made, the government wants them to be made and taxed in Britain, rather than for the technology to be exploited elsewhere. Scenario Two again.

I have already mentioned climate change as perhaps the starkest example of the Tragedy of the Commons. It has of course already been the subject of a series of world conferences, of which Kyoto in December 1997 was supposed to be the focal point. A surprisingly large reduction of 7% of greenhouse gases below 1990 levels by 2012 was agreed – even by the United States. These targets however fell far short of the IPCC scientific recommendations mentioned in the last chapter. However, even these modest proposals failed when the arrangements should have been finalized in November 2000. The USA, Japan, Australia and Canada wrecked them by proposing a formula unacceptable to the rest of the world whereby by counting existing forests within their borders, they could in effect continue business (i.e. expansion) as usual. Finally, President George W. Bush repudiated the Kyoto agreement anyway.

There are three specific areas of concern against which all others pale into insignificance: the oil industry, air traffic, and rainforest destruction. In the case of the oil industry, although the same pressures are clearly at work, there is a gleam of hope that it will be less intractable than most examples of the 'Tragedy'. If governments really do start to take their Kyoto commitments seriously, a shift to renewable sources of energy could happen relatively quickly.

It has been estimated that the fuel consumption and exhaust produced by each and every plane carrying passengers from Britain to Australia is the same as if each of those passengers had driven a car for the same distance. But much of that pollution is water vapour and greenhouse gases in the stratosphere which was previously devoid of them. As there is no rain at that altitude, these accumulate, and will take years to dissipate. If this single cause of global warming could be curbed, we may indeed have a longer breathing space to deal with all other forms of economic growth.

But no. Despite the scientific evidence, governments continue to subsidize airlines, so that anyone who does not fly on environmental grounds subsidizes those who do. This is a straightforward case of Scenario Two, with the USA again in the role of Bernard. Other countries remonstrated, but naturally, their rational response to the USA's refusal was not to put themselves at a disadvantage. The rationalizations employed during the fisheries disaster were being writ large. Airlines not only offer cheaper fares than surface travel, an environmental scandal in itself, but all are in fierce competition with cheap fares as the selling point. This huge area for pollution reduction was not even mentioned at Kyoto. On the contrary, just as with fish processing capacity, increases are still planned.

In the same vein, the USA has probably the cheapest petrol prices in the world. So it stood out at Kyoto against tighter targets. At least Europe had made some attempt to introduce environmental factors into fuel prices, hence the backlash, but there has never been the slightest question of such a move in the USA. The reason is of course that no politician dare suggest otherwise as long as 'Bernards' heavily outnumber 'Alfreds' there, which they clearly do, for reasons which I shall discuss in Chapter 5. Meanwhile, efforts to reduce greenhouse gases elsewhere are nullified.

Rainforest destruction speaks for itself. There are comprehensive accounts already in existence of the appalling scale and speed of this. Not only is it a prime example of the Tragedy of the Commons, it is yet another illustration of how Scenario One inevitably deepens into Scenario Two. The rainforest is a crucial part of the biosphere which affects us all. There are two factors in the destruction of the rainforest – transnational companies, and subsistence farmers on the margins who do it simply to survive for another year. The transnationals claim that in Brazil it is poor farmers who are responsible for more of the damage than they are. This is of course no excuse, but there is a grain of truth in it. Both problems must be addressed if hopes of an ecologically sustainable future are to become a reality.

Quite apart from specific examples, the 'Tragedy' is driving the whole dynamic of globalization. Some of us are appalled at the rapacity with which mega corporations are sucking the life out of peoples without the power to resist, not to mention the ecosphere, and the specious arguments used to justify such behaviour. But what would be the point of one or more of them giving up their hard fought advantage, if the way is simply cleared for the next wave of predators?

The following extract is taken from *The 2020 Challenge* by Duane Elgin.[6] Chapter 6, 'An evolutionary crash and bounce', outlines two true accounts. The first is the story of Rapanui (Easter Island), an awesome real example of a Scenario Two worst case. In Part Two I shall return to the second, the story of Gaviotas, a village in Colombia which shows just what can be achieved against the odds with a clear vision of a sustainable society.

The human experience on Easter Island provides a stunning example of both an ecological and an evolutionary crash. Only 150 square miles in area, it is located in one of the most remote places on Earth — in the Pacific Ocean, roughly 2,000 miles off the coast of South America. The first Europeans to visit the island were the crew of a Dutch ship that arrived on Easter Sunday in 1722 — hence the name Easter Island. They found a primitive society of approximately 3,000 people, living in wretched reed huts and caves, engaged in almost perpetual warfare, and resorting to cannibalism in a desperate attempt to supplement the meager food supplies available on the tree-less island. What was most amazing to the Dutch, the island was covered with more than 600 massive stone statues, each averaging more than 20 feet in height, which indicated that an advanced society had once flourished on Easter Island. To the Europeans, the primi-tive, barbaric, and poverty-stricken people of the island did not seem capable of the complex tasks of carving, transporting, and erecting so many statues. The story of Easter Island's decline is a chilling warning regarding the consequences of irreversibly damaging the environment.

Archeological evidence reveals that when Easter Island was first settled by a few dozen Polynesian colonists in approximately 500 A.D., it had a mild climate and volcanic soil, was covered by forests, and was filled with animal and plant life (although there were relatively few species, given the remoteness of the island). Among the foods that the settlers brought with them, yams and chickens were particularly suited to the climate and soil. As the islanders prospered, their numbers grew to an estimated 7,000, when the population peaked in 1550.

Because food production was so easy, the islanders had abundant free time to devote to elaborate rituals and statue building. Over a thousand years, they developed one of the most advanced and com-plex societies in the world, despite their limited resources and tech-nologies. From early on, however, they used the resources of the island beyond its regenerative capacity. Archeological evidence shows that the destruction of the island's forests was well underway by the year 800 — only 300 years after settlers first arrived. By the 1500s, the forests and palm trees had disappeared as people cleared land for agriculture, and used the surviving trees to build ocean-going canoes, burn as firewood, build homes, and transport statues. At the end, the remaining forests disappeared quickly, as the islanders apparently used logs to transport statues in a competitive rivalry between the clans to see who could build the most. The loss of the tree cover increased soil erosion and reduced soil quality — and both factors reduced crop yields.

The ecological destruction was not confined to the forests. Jared Diamond, professor of medicine at UCLA, describes how the animal life was also eradicated:

> The destruction of the island's animals was as extreme as that of the forests: without exception, every species of native land bird became extinct. Even shellfish were over exploited, until people had to settle for small sea snails. . . . Porpoise bones disappeared abruptly from the garbage heaps around 1500; no one could harpoon porpoises anymore, since the trees used for constructing the big seagoing canoes no longer existed. . . .
>
> By the mid 1500s, the biosphere was so devastated that it was beyond short-term recovery. With the forests gone, ocean fishing was impossible without trees to build boats. With animals hunted to extinction, the people turned on one another. Centralized authority broke down, and the island descended into chaos, with rival clans living in caves and competing with one another for survival.

Eventually, according to Diamond, the islanders "turned to the largest remaining meat source available: humans, whose bones became common in late Easter Island garbage heaps. Oral traditions of the islanders are rife with cannibalism." By 1700, the population had crashed to between one-quarter and one-tenth of its former level.

Professor Diamond concludes that the parallels between Easter Island and the Earth are strong. "Easter Island is Earth writ small. Today, again, a rising population confronts shrinking resources. . . . we can no more escape into space than the Easter Islanders could flee into the ocean.

Paradoxically, for me the most worrying aspect of this threat to mankind lies with those who are trying to respond to it. It is not clear that the Green movement fully recognizes the significance of the Tragedy of the Commons, especially the sheer enormity of the dynamics driving Scenario Two – the principle that in general the worse the ecological behaviour the greater the perpetrator's economic strength in conventional terms. Schumacher's dictum was "Think globally, act locally".[7] Perhaps the latter half is better observed than the former because it is only at the local level that Greens can have a significant impact, certainly in Britain. Of course decentralization is right in principle. Decisions should be taken as locally as possible, and individuals should feel empowered, not controlled. But how are we to dovetail these ideals with the need for 'mutual coercion mutually agreed upon' – worldwide?[8]

This is clearly a huge problem. Certainly localization and carbon taxes as outlined by Colin Hines have a vital part to play.[9,10] Does it entail some form of democratically elected *world* government, with effective powers of enforcement? If so, then most aspects are beyond the scope of this book, which merely offers a possible basis for a worldwide consensus. How might such a government arise? Are there lessons in the experience of the European Union? How are the disastrous influences of the IMF, WTO or the World Bank to be circumvented? Gaia has always successfully re-established equilibrium after environmental disturbances without any vestige of world government, but we have yet to learn how she does it, or whether her methods would be acceptable in the context of human society. But somehow we must achieve Garrett Hardin's prescription. Until this is in prospect, what hope can there be of those who do not share the Green paradigm taking any notice? They will go on demanding cheap petrol, over-fishing, building entertainment and shopping complexes, selling arms, expanding car (and other consumer durable) sales, exploring for oil (and flaring off the inconvenient bits into the stratosphere), promoting air travel and felling rainforest for profit *until it is too late*.

For anyone who still has difficulty in taking this threat seriously, please read *A Green History of the World*, by Clive Ponting.[11] The Tragedy is not inevitable, but a theme which I shall develop is that the whole of the human race (except a tiny minority) has been on a course of expansion ever since the introduction of permanent agriculture. For all except that pre-agricultural minority, the Tragedy has been a constant threat requiring progressively more difficult evasive action, not always successful.

As we have seen, the Tragedy can operate at any level, from the personal to the global, but it is in the context of globalization that the Tragedy becomes devastating. Wherever there is unrestricted competition, each competitor must disregard the long term common good if it conflicts with his immediate interests. The rule is whatever the risk, it is outweighed by that of losing market share. The first competitor to throw in his hand in this deadly poker school ensures not that the world will be preserved, but that others will gain at his expense. If primary resources are added to Garrett Hardin's population and pollution, everything else comes down to these three basics. Sooner or later each must come uncomfortably close to the limits of its 'carrying capacity', and with the exponential principle at work, the moment will, as we have seen in the examples where it has already happened, tend to come rather more suddenly than conventional wisdom anticipates.

As expansion comes up against limits, the Tragedy ensures that unless there is a better strategy in place, each participant can see no alternative but to hasten and worsen the crisis. This book attempts to suggest such a strategy. It is possible that the fishermen off the east coast of North America and the Easter Islanders were more stupid than the rest of us. But is it not just as probable that like us, including even some who are trying to take evasive action, they simply underestimated the speed with which the exponential principle finally snaps shut the trap set by the Tragedy of the Commons?

Notes and References

1   Hardin, Garrett (1968), 'The Tragedy of the Commons', *Science* 162 (1968), pp1243-1248.
2   An actual example of this occurred in 1999 when the British pig industry was subjected to regulations which did not apply to imported products.
3   'The Spanish,' says WWF's fisheries expert Michael Sutton, 'are well known as an outlaw fishing nation and one of the most overcapitalised fleets in the world.' One Spanish multinational corporation now owns a global network of some 30 companies in 18 nations of Africa, Asia and Latin America. Quoted from Dick Russell, Internet posting.
4   Brubaker, Elisabeth, *Cod don't vote. How politics destroyed Atlantic Canada's fisheries*. An Internet discussion. Email ElisabethBrubaker@ nextcity.com or PerspectiveCDV@nextcity.com.
5   Opinion polls put public support for the blockades at 88% in France, and between 78% and 84% in Britain.
6   The 2020 Challenge, by Duane Elgin. 6. Two Scenarios: An evolu-

tionary crash and bounce. Internet website: www.newhorizons.org/ph_elgin2020f.html (Note: this website appears to have been discontinued.)

7   Schumacher, E. F. (1973), *Small is Beautiful: Economics as If People Really Mattered*, Abacus, London.

8   See Axelrod, Robert (1984), *The Evolution of Cooperation*, Basic Books, New York for a discussion of this topic.

9   Hines, Colin (2000), *Localiztion – A Global Manifesto*, Earthscan, London.

10   Hines, Colin (2000), *From Seattle to Nice: challenging the Free Trade agenda at the heart of enlargement*. A paper prepared for Caroline Lucas MEP, published privately by Hines and Lucas.

11   Ponting, Clive (1991), *A Green History of the World*, Sinclair Stevenson, London.

III

Racism and the environmental crisis

Why we must act *before* the problems become urgent

There have been attempts to rubbish scientific warnings against continuing 'business as usual'. These have been welcomed by those who think they have most to lose, but that is not surprising in the light of the Tragedy of the Commons. What really terrifies me is the view that Green proposals may only come into their own when the consequences of not adopting them begin to bite. If we wait for trouble, the precedents suggest that that is exactly what we shall get. Racism has not up to now been closely associated with environmental issues. Yet xenophobia is the mainspring of a whole spectrum of responses ranging from individual acts of racism through full-scale warfare up to and including genocide. It is for me what in computer jargon would be called a 'default setting' – an automatic response in certain circumstances if no other arrangements have been made. These circumstances self-evidently include ecological problems. Whenever shortages, or for that matter surpluses occur people will either share, or compete for whatever is available. Competition may well be a reasonable way to allocate a surplus. Any animal that lives in groups will compete as a group. That is all that is needed as a basis for xenophobia.[1] In times of perceived plenty, racism should not be a major problem, but it will be there, lurking in the subconscious just in case it is needed. It seems axiomatic to me that unless more constructive solutions have been put in place in good time, xenophobia must be a component in any response to shortages or insecurity.

The rise of Nazism could be an example of resource issues having a close connection with actual occurrences of racism, but the countries in Europe which currently have the strongest parties using xenophobic rhetoric are also among the most comfortable economically. In Britain, racist attacks – or at least reports of them – have been increasing as unemployment declines. But all these up to date examples must be set against the background of increasing competitiveness and insecurity engendered by the dominant neo-liberal paradigm. Other factors may play a part in the actual incidence of racism, but I believe that there are formidable reasons why it features prominently, both as a fact of life and as a major worry for those of us who deplore it, and why above all it is relevant to the question of ecological limits.

It is perfectly obvious why a tiger is a killer, or why a wasp has a sting. They are products of evolution. Any innate trait among humans is likely to be there because it has or has had some survival value. Of course, in humans innate traits are inextricably bound up with cultural constructs and traditions. I argue only that there is evidence of innate 'hard-wired' components at the root of xenophobia.

But we are all different. Just as we differ in obvious traits, so we must be presumed to be different in less visible ways. Some individuals are clearly racist as a major feature of their outlook on life, regardless of circumstances. At the opposite end of the spectrum, in others this trait will be absent, even in circumstances where they personally would be better off. I hope for example that Greens would regard racist ways of rationing abhorrent under any circumstances. In between, I believe that the attitude of the population as a whole will sway back and forth, depending on a wide variety of circumstances.

Anyone in competition for a resource perceived to be too scarce to meet everyone's needs will at some point at least *think* along the lines of belonging to a group with a better claim, or perhaps just a stronger group. In a society which is well organized, and running its affairs efficiently and wisely, the instances when this temptation might occur would be reduced to a minimum. In the animal kingdom, where we might assume that planning is unlikely, the reduction of conflicts between members of the same species over resources of all kinds is well organized and reasonably efficient. There may be fighting to establish 'pecking order' and territorial boundaries, though most species have evolved displays as a way of minimizing mutually harmful violence. Once in place, they decide who gets what without further bloodshed.

It would be unwise to believe that we could ignore ecological limits, or permanently conquer disease, or any other of the unnatural overweening claims which tended to be the hallmark of the twentieth century. I believe that unless a compelling case to the contrary can be made, we would do well to recognize and accept that 'default settings' found in the animal kingdom will apply to us until we work out viable alternatives. For this reason I believe that two lines of enquiry have some important and sobering lessons for us: research on chimpanzees, and on their close relatives the bonobos. Contrary to the original classification whereby the great apes were thought to be a closely related group to which humans were distantly related, DNA evidence now suggests that humans, chimpanzees and bonobos are more closely related to each other than any of them are to other apes.

Jane Goodall started a research project on wild chimpanzees in the Gombe Reserve in Tanzania in 1960. She is still there in 2003. In 1986 she wrote a comprehensive account of her work, drawing also on work on chimpanzees by others, in her book *The Chimpanzees of Gombe – Patterns of Behaviour*.[2] What emerges is that although chimpanzees are very different from us, they show striking similarities, some of which are extremely unnerving.

Jane Goodall admits that if her study had terminated after ten years as originally envisaged, our understanding of them would have been woefully deficient. Until 1972 it had been possible to portray the Gombe chimpanzees as gentle, and free from the worst human traits. They had turned out to be more like us in their behaviour than we thought, and a good deal more intelligent than we had given them credit for. They use and construct tools. Other studies have shown that although they are anatomically incapable of speech, they *can* use sign language, even teaching it to their young, and using it in emergency situations where one would expect instinctive reactions to take over. They are capable of complex emotions, caring for their young almost as long, and certainly just as lovingly as we do. They comfort each other when ill or grieving and their gestures in these situations or when greeting old friends are uncannily 'human'.

It was in 1970 that Jane Goodall and her team first noticed that the chimpanzee community they were observing was no longer homogeneous. By 1972 it had split into two hostile camps, which she called the Kasakela and Kahama communities, based on the valleys they inhabited. Attacks by the Kasakela began in January 1974, and by November 1977, the Kahama community was no more. The annihilation (Jane Goodall's word) took the form of a series of attacks by groups of Kasakela males on individual members of the Kahama group, waiting as necessary until they caught each one alone.

Of the five males in the Kahama community, the fatal attacks on three of them were actually observed. The body of a fourth was found in circumstances conclusively indicating the same cause.[3] The fifth male had simply disappeared. During the same four year period, at least two healthy males from the Kasakela community disappeared without explanation, so it is possible that they did not have things entirely their own way.

At first it was hoped that this was aberrant behaviour caused by feeding to attract the chimpanzees, since this had been observed to increase aggression within the group at the research centre. There was however some evidence that another group, the Kalande, behaved in the same way towards the Kasakela community between 1977 and 1981, though with less drastic results. The Kalande community, living further away to the south, did not discover the Gombe banana source until 1982, when they had not only taken over the now vacant Kahama valley, but had invaded deep into Kasakela territory. They were still not habituated to humans, and the bananas could not have been responsible for their behaviour. Two able-bodied Kasakela males disappeared, and one female was badly wounded, in the south of the Kasakela range. Jane Goodall also quotes accumulating evidence from several other researchers that this behaviour is typical rather than exceptional, but not among bonobos, who are now accepted as a distinct species. It does however seem to occur in episodes, with periods of 'peace' lasting for up to twenty years or possibly longer.

These attacks are completely different from the aggression and fights which take place within a group. These are rare enough for Jane Goodall to say:

Early field studies of chimpanzees (including my own) gave rise to the myth of the gentle, peace-loving ape. As more data on chimpanzee behaviour have been collected over the years, at Gombe and elsewhere, this myth has gradually been dispelled.

Although dominance fights for the 'alpha' position can be quite serious, by 1986, after 25 years of observation at Gombe, a slightly shorter field study at nearby Mahale, and a total of over 14 years at a number of other locations there had been no known deaths from this cause among wild chimpanzees. Two such deaths have been recorded amongst groups in captivity, where the antagonists were evenly matched and where conditions could not by definition be natural. Disabling or permanent injury is rare, and the fight *always* stops when one submits. One particularly sobering aspect of the extermination of the Kahama chimpanzees was that their killers were close kin, and had been in normal social contact less than five years before the first fatal attack.

Why do they do it? The obvious effect is twofold: it reduces the overall population, which otherwise slowly expands, and it increases the ratio of females to males, because whereas *all* males are killed if possible, only older females meet the same fate. Younger females either join the aggressor community (duress may or may not be necessary, but it has been observed) or sometimes they escape to another. Although other factors, notably disease are significant, inter-group attacks seem to be a major factor in maintaining a stable population level.[4]

However, there is still a puzzle to be explained. This particular form of behaviour is unique to chimpanzees – unless one draws the uncomfortable parallel with mankind. All other social animals – even the bonobos, of whom more later in this chapter – have evolved ways of competing with each other so that they stay within the carrying capacity of their environment but without such 'proto-warfare' (Jane Goodall's description). Baboons, whilst more distantly related than chimpanzees, live in more highly organized communities, and they also live generally in more open savannah type grassland where our ancestors are believed to have evolved. Fights occur, especially at territorial limits, but not murderous raids into neighbouring territory. Just why chimpanzees have evolved such a self-destructive pattern is not clear, but as Jane Goodall points out:

> In the course of evolution natural selection has ruthlessly eliminated behaviours that have led to reduced levels of survival and reproductive success…[though]…neutral behaviour will be tolerated.[5]

So the chances are that there are sound reasons for the development of racism among chimpanzees.

On reading these detailed accounts of inter-community violence, I was first of all forcibly reminded of the kind of racial attack of which the murder of Stephen Lawrence in April 1993 was a prime example, but which is clearly far from isolated. The obvious enthusiasm with which late adolescent and young adult chimpanzee males engage in these aggressive co-operative forays is remarkably similar to the behaviour of organized football crowd troublemakers at away matches. Some may dismiss these comparisons as far-fetched. At all events Jane Goodall does not think chimpanzee behaviour is irrelevant to humans. For me, it is the fact that chimpanzees show so many other quasi-human traits that makes their xenophobic behaviour especially disturbing.[6] As Goodall infers, chimpanzees come as close to organized warfare as is possible for an animal without language. My own position is that unless a case to the contrary can be made, it would be wise to assume at the outset that chimpanzee behaviour is unlikely to be far removed from our own 'default settings'. Let us examine how far we have progressed from our chimpanzee relatives.

We no longer kill members of another group on principle. Well, most of us that is, for most of the time. At least race attacks and genocide are regarded with disgust by those not involved, and they are no longer the norm. Oh dear! Even that statement has to be qualified. Remember, even chimps leave their neighbours alone for years at a time. Among humans, long periods of peace occur between quite large populations, though not wherever two groups who define themselves as different occupy the same territory. So at best we seem to be talking about a difference in degree rather than a difference in kind.

The English for example have a self-stereotype of giving as good as they get if attacked, but of being peace-loving if left alone. When the Romans left Britain in the fifth century, what is now England was entirely Welsh speaking. Just why the Celtic language was confined to Cumbria, Wales and Cornwall by the time of the Domesday Book in 1086 is not known in detail, but it seems unlikely to have been a voluntary process. Irish history casts doubt on the English self-image, and the original inhabitants of Tasmania would also beg to differ – if any had survived. Similarly the annexation of North and South America by Europeans should undermine any feeling of superiority by those who feel that they, or people like them, could never have been responsible for the atrocities of the Second World War, or in the Balkans, or Rwanda.

However, even in the 'worst case scenario' – that humankind really is prone to intervals of warfare, and possibly even genocide.- there are measures we can take to reduce their occurrence. It simply becomes important to do so *in good time*. We must do so *before* we run into the environmental buffers, when competition over resources will sharpen intensely. Social, job and cash restrictions will re-activate latent racism so that the search for alternatives to violence will be too late.

Fortunately there are some clues that we may not actually be quite so vicious. The worst excesses among humans seem to have been during times of change, and specifically of expansion. Of course recorded history consists largely of continuous change and expansion, but it is easy to overlook the fact that many human groups did not take part in this expansion and were less prone to warfare. In Australia for example prior to the arrival of Europeans, a pattern of peaceful contact between tribes had evolved which seems to have been stable for several millennia. In parts of New Guinea there was a tradition of inter-tribal fighting stopping as soon as *one* person was killed. An Inuit (Eskimo) on being told about the

Second World War then raging elsewhere, exclaimed: "You mean you kill people you don't even know?!!"

Having drawn on our nearest animal relatives to sound a warning, the same area of investigation offers some grounds for cautious optimism. Chimpanzees may offer evidence for a 'hard-wired' basis to racism, but there is equally cogent evidence for a very different approach to resource sharing: the bonobos. At first sight bonobos look like chimps, but there are anatomical differences, and their social life and group structure are very different. They live in an area of rainforest separated from chimpanzees by the Zaire (Congo) River. There are estimated to be no more than 10,000 in the wild. They have been studied in the wild since the mid 1970s, and there are several colonies in zoos. According to Frans de Waal, chimpanzees and bonobos are believed to have diverged later than humans from the common ancestor, so that they are equally closely related to humans. De Waal surmises that of the three, it is bonobos who are likely to have changed the least.[7]

Sex other than for procreation is the salient feature of bonobo society. However, the relevance to the present discussion is that bonobos have a way of de-fusing conflict situations without violence. They are the epitome of the saying "make love not war". Within the group, violence is virtually unknown. Furthermore, according to De Waal:

> Serious conflict between bonobo groups has been witnessed in the field, but it seems quite rare. On the contrary, reports exist of peaceable mingling, including mutual sex and grooming, between what appear to be different communities.[7]

This is something which under no circumstances happens among chimpanzees. The other major feature of bonobo society is the independence of the females. De Waal describes them as dominant, despite being physically the weaker sex, but his account leads me to modify that description. Unlike chimpanzees, where all adult males dominate and subjugate all females with gratuitous violence, female bonobos do not seem to bother to 'dominate' their males. All they do is to gang up in twos (or more, though that is not normally necessary) to ensure that their will prevails. However they always use group solidarity to take precedence at a food source. In any case, any tense situation is normally resolved by mutual sex, followed as often as not by the possessor of a resource sharing it amicably. It is females who form close bonds rather than males. Bonobos have no need of the male 'war party' which is essential to chimpanzees, if only out of pre-emptive self-defence. Despite the frequency of sex, the bonobo reproduction rate is no higher than chimpanzees. Why is not clear, but their population appears to remain stable – without killing each other!

Bonobos are as closely related to us as are chimpanzees, so that any lessons for humans to be drawn from them are just as valid. Feminists who challenge family life as bound up with male dominance, stressing instead female solidarity and the peaceful resolution of conflicts, could equally claim a 'hard wired' basis for their view. Whether a trait is 'good' or 'bad' depends at least partly on whether it is still relevant or obsolete. What follows is conjecture, but I hope that it will be useful as the starting point of a much needed discussion.

I believe that there is an explanation for the different strategies found among chimpanzees and bonobos which is mirrored in similar choices by humans as they spread around the globe. According to De Waal:

> Divergence of the chimpanzee and the bonobo lines [was] perhaps prompted by the chimpanzee's need to adapt to relatively open, dry habitats [see 'East Side Story: The Origin of Humankind', by Yves Coppens; *Scientific American*, May 1994]. In contrast, bonobos probably never left the protection of the trees.[7]

In other words, the chimpanzees, unlike the bonobos, had been extending their range. The chimpanzees have a strategy which is robust, and would ensure better chances of survival where competition for resources is an issue: not only expansion, where it originated, but also in 'Tragedy of the Commons' episodes, to which expansion must always be vulnerable.

It would not be difficult to guess which human groups would be at an advantage (or at less of a disadvantage) if the exponential principle does take us by surprise. Imagine the likely outcome if a group of chimpanzees, with their approach to strangers, met a group of bonobos, with theirs. Aggressors would tend to oust conciliators – a clear example of the Tragedy of the Commons. Humans have been expanding for at least 100,000 years. Some, so-called primitive tribes opted out of this expansion, and returned to a state of equilibrium with their environment. More recently, aggressive or technologically advanced peoples have been displacing societies which had no need to be because they were in harmony with their environment – the Tragedy again. For most of humankind, the whole of recorded history and some considerable period before has consisted of expansion and change, and hiccups in 'progress'.

It is possible that chimpanzees and bonobos have chosen conflict-based and conflict-*resolution*-based strategies respectively precisely because the former had been extending their range whereas the latter had adapted to a stable environment. It is no coincidence that the bonobos have a strategy which would suit a 'space capsule' Earth extremely well. Fortunately there are, or at least have been, human societies which chose a similar path.

But how far should we go towards the bonobo model? Couples co-operating to bring up children should be compatible with peaceful conflict resolution, but we shall presumably have to find some mechanism other than indiscriminate sex. Pair bonding obviously has some value. We are not the only species to have stumbled on it, but it does rely on the assumption that the father is supporting his own children. I believe there is DNA evidence among birds that fidelity within a pair is a working myth rather than a reality, but would this prove helpful in the modern human context? But there is a grain of truth in the feminist critique. Male dominance has traditionally played a major part in cementing the nuclear family. If society were to insist on that as the only acceptable unit, it might be difficult to deny that male opinions still dominate. However there is no reason to go to the other extreme and ditch the family entirely. After all, chimpanzees demonstrate that racism and male domination can exist without family life. The present western norm of the family still being seen as the preferable option, but with an opt-out so that no one need feel trapped, seems to me perfectly consistent with an ecologically sustainable society. However, the theme which I shall develop in later chapters does indicate that the family may not be the appropriate primary economic unit.

There are of course other factors likely to come into play in response to worsening ecological pressures. For example, governments might become more authoritarian in an attempt to impose unpopular solutions. I shall discuss in later chapters why I think these would (will?) fail. I have focused on racism, or more accurately the xenophobic roots of racism, because I believe the implications are unavoidable.

I cannot stress too strongly the importance of putting ecological solutions in place *well before* the need becomes too pressing. If a crisis has to occur before Green solutions are feasible, atavistic reactions will take over, and they will owe more to the chimpanzee (racist) than the bonobo (conflict-resolution-oriented) side of our nature. In other words, frightened or deprived people are far more likely to listen to racist demagoguery than co-operative solutions. There is worrying evidence that this is already happening.[8] Another theme which I shall develop in the course of this book is that co-operation entails social justice. Even without the facts outlined in this chapter, it should be self-evident that the less social justice there is, the more extreme the fascism which will gain credence.

I believe that we humans are on a cusp between two very different primal 'default settings' capable of responding to ecological limitations. If one accepts that genetic predisposition and environmental factors are interactive, which we shall choose depends on the environment we create for ourselves – growth oriented or sustainable. Bearing in mind how suddenly the Tragedy of the Commons sometimes strikes, the line of least resistance – believing critics of scientific warnings of ecological damage – begins to look irresponsible. But the Easter Islanders demonstrate not only how easy it is to ignore ample warning of trouble, but also the form that trouble may take. Any conflict carries the potential to reach a point where a war mentality takes over from more constructive responses. If we persist too long with unsustainable attempts at growth, so that it is the aggressive 'default setting' which is activated, any further debate will be pointless.

Notes and References

1   For a discussion of the origins and dynamics of xenophobia, see Hardin, Garrett (1977), *The Limits of Altruism*, Indiana University Press.

2   Goodall, Jane (1986), *The Chimpanzees of Gombe*, Harvard University Press.

3.   The fourth victim was found 'with multiple wounds ... similar to those sustained by the victims of inter-community fights' (*The Chimpanzees of Gombe*, p510). The area had been searched because local fishermen had told the Gombe research team that they had heard fierce fighting two days earlier, followed by the passage close to them of a group of chimpanzees. (This indicates that they must have been Kasakela chimpanzees – only they, or the Kahama, were familiar with humans. Any others would have avoided them.)

4   There was one other bizarre mechanism. From 1974 to 1977, one female and her daughter were seen to kill three infants from their own community, and were believed to be responsible for the unexplained disappearance of up to seven others (*The Chimpanzees of Gombe*, p78). There is however no corroboration of this behaviour in any other chimpanzee group, wild or in captivity, so whether it was normal or pathological is unclear. It stopped when the female gave birth herself.

5   *The Chimpanzees of Gombe*, p198.

6   Another uncomfortable resonance with human behaviour (unlike other animals, including bonobos) observed by Jane Goodall was that whenever a male chimpanzee was possessive of a female, he *always* attacked her, never rivals.

7   De Waal, Frans B. M., 'Bonobo Sex and Society'. Originally published in *Scientific American*, March 1995, pp82-88 Available at www.sciam.com

8   In the 2001 General Election, the British National Party polled an average of 12.95% in three constituencies, Burnley, Oldham East and Oldham West. Riots with a racial element had taken place just before the election in one town, and occurred just after the election in the other. Growing opposition to asylum seekers also points in the same direction.

— Part Two —

A Way Out?

IV

What is possible

Precedents for a sustainable world

It doesn't have to be like Easter Island. Duane Elgin's second example is the village of Gaviotas.[1] It could be the first example of what I shall call Scenario Three. Could it be that all we have to do is scale it up?

A striking example of an evolutionary bounce is the village of Gaviotas, located on the grassy plains of eastern Colombia in South America. Established in the midst of a vast, desolate plain, where nothing but a few nutrient-poor grasses grow, it is surely one of our planet's least desirable areas to live. Paolo Lugari, who founded the village in 1971, explained why the villagers chose this site: 'They always put social experiments in the easiest, most fertile places. We wanted the hardest place. We figured if we could do it here [in the most resource-starved region in the country], we could do it anywhere.' When people told him that the area was 'just a big, wet desert,' he would reply, 'The only deserts are deserts of the imagination.' In the space of a single generation — roughly 30 years — Gaviotans have created a sustainable economy, nurturing community, and flourishing ecosystem.

In the early 1970s, Lugari brought scientists, engineers, doctors, university students, and others to this remote and inhospitable site to explore how it could be transformed into a thriving community. They produced a dazzling array of low-cost but highly efficient technologies. For example, to pump water, they created a light-weight windmill whose blades are contoured, like the wings of an airplane, so they can trap the soft breezes of the equator. They attached highly efficient water pumps to see-saws so that when children were playing, they were simultaneously pumping water for the community. Solar water heaters were invented that could catch the diffuse energy of the sun even on the many cloudy days. Underground ducts were placed in hillsides to provide natural air-conditioning for their hospital. Photovoltaic cells on roof-tops provide electricity. Some food is grown in hydroponic gardens.

The transformation of the local ecosystem has been as remarkable as the development of innovative technologies. Since the early 1980s, the Gaviotans have planted roughly two million Caribbean pine trees, the only tree that would grow in the nearly toxic soil. This created more than 20,000 acres of forest. From the trees, the villagers harvest and sell pine resin, which is used in the manufacture of paint, turpentine, and paper. This provides a source of income for the community. The pine forest has brought fresh nutrients to the soil, cooled the ground, slowed the wind, and raised the humidity. In turn, these changes have allowed dormant seeds of native trees to sprout and grow. The sheltering pine trees are enabling a diverse, indigenous forest to regenerate itself with surprising speed. As a result, the local populations of deer, anteater, and other animals are growing. The Gaviotans have decided to allow the indigenous forest to overtake and choke out the pine forest over the next century, enabling the area to return to its original state as an extension of the Amazon.

The Gaviotans have been equally inventive socially. Everyone earns the same salary, which is above minimum wage. Many of the basics of life are free, including housing, health care, food, and schooling for the children. With no poverty, there has been no need for police or a jail. Government is by consensus and unwritten rules of common sense. Dogs, pesticides, and guns are not allowed. Alcohol use is confined to homes. Loafers are not tolerated. The harvest from this community of social invention is a village where people exude happiness. The people of Gaviotas have the confidence of a sustainable future, a strong community, meaningful work, and a peaceful life.

As the village grows, its creator envisions new satellite villages. 'I see enclaves of maybe twenty families, little satellites surrounding Gaviotas, no more than twenty minutes away by bicycle.' He envisions 'little island communities where people live in productive harmony with nature and technology. And with each other.'

Alan Weisman, in his book *Gaviotas: A Village to Reinvent the World*, beautifully summarizes the net result of the Gaviotans' efforts:

Surrounded by a land seen either as empty or plagued with misery, they had forged a way and a peace they believed could prosper long after the last drop of the earth's petroleum was burned away. They were so small, but their hope was great enough to brighten the planet turning beneath them no matter how much their fellow humans seemed bent on wrecking it. Against all skeptics and odds, Gaviotas had lighted a path through a magnificent but darkened land, whose sorrows mirrored a beautiful, embattled world.

Too good to be true? Perhaps it will be a little more difficult than just scaling it up. Whilst it is reassuring to have a working example, Gaviotas is not my preferred blueprint for a sustainable world. There is an immediately obvious problem in that the Gaviotans started from scratch, and the participants were self-selected, and therefore unanimously committed to the project from the outset. So long as that remains the case, and so long as their population stays within the carrying capacity of their environment, and provided no neighbours, or neighbouring conflicts encroach, the Tragedy of the Commons will not happen to them. They may not be safe from a global Tragedy though. But the majority of the world's population cannot start afresh in a desert, and most of us don't want to. I just want to stay where I am, but with the rules and aims of society geared towards sustainability. As I hope to make clear shortly, I even believe that such an ambition could become widespread, unlikely as that may seem at the moment. What we need is a way of getting to grips with the dynamics of the Tragedy of the Commons before the conflict based default setting takes over, and solves resource issues by attrition.

Fortunately the precedents are not uniformly pessimistic. One can even assert that the history of Easter Island is no more typical than that of Gaviotas. The vast majority of so-called primitive societies were in or close to ecological equilibrium prior to disturbance by Europeans. The danger arises from the fact that Easter Island was a special case which unfortunately bears more resemblance to historical, recent and current global developments than do any of the more optimistic examples. How did the others do it? What can we learn from them?

Along with *The Tragedy of the Commons*, another seminal influence at a time when my personal paradigm was undergoing a drastic shift was a book called *Poverty and Progress* by Richard G. Wilkinson.[2] His thesis, as described on the back cover, was as follows:

Richard Wilkinson demonstrates that the pursuit of progress is not the real driving force behind change. He argues that economic development is simply the escape route of societies caught in the ecological pincers of population growth and scarce resources. The things we think of as the fruits of man's search for progress … such as … increasingly sophisticated technology … are part of the struggle to keep up with the growing productive task created by ecological pressures. In this light, primitive societies appear less poor than we imagine, and advanced ones less rich.

In Chapter 3, Wilkinson outlines the norm of ecological equilibrium. He first explains mechanisms by which animals achieve this, and goes on to give examples of pre-industrial human societies whose cultural patterns perform this function. A major point which he makes is that starvation – or even shortages as other than isolated, exceptional features – are unknown in either animal or human populations *except where they are in the course of transition*, normally following some disturbance in their environment. The implications of the last sentence are quite staggering, so I repeat: poverty is extremely rare in undisturbed populations. Although Malthus' theory that starvation was the effective check on the size of populations is now generally discredited, Wilkinson accepts that this is indeed the case *in changing or disturbed societies*.[3] All undisturbed populations have somehow found a limiting mechanism which normally allows a standard of living comfortably above the minimum for all their members.

If dumb animals and supposedly ignorant savages can do this with minimal resources and technology, something must be seriously wrong with an advanced, technologically sophisticated society which cannot. I personally believe that there is an inability rather than a refusal to eradicate poverty. This is not a simple matter of greed, or of those with wealth not caring about the rest. Many 'haves' do indeed rationalize the poverty of others as 'their own fault', but even if this never happened, I believe that the paradox of poverty in a world of plenty would still exist. It is the sharing strategy which is at the root of the problem. A society can consciously choose a sharing strategy, indeed it is the theme of this book that our society must do just that – globally. I shall explore what that strategy should be in the course of this and the next chapter. But for most of the time in most societies that choice is effectively unconscious and driven by inertia, i.e. tradition. The sharing (more accurately not sharing) strategy current in Britain (for example) is patently malfunctioning. The circumstances in which it developed and suited our ancestors – gradual expansion into pastures new – no longer apply. Greed and selfishness are as much symptoms of the insecurity endemic in Western society as causes of it.

Wilkinson sets out certain core features commonly found in societies in or near ecological equilibrium:

> Some societies limit their populations *consciously* to prevent food shortages. Others however limit them in relation to a scarcity of other goods associated with prestige and status which have nothing to do with subsistence. Competition for essential resources is replaced by competition for socially valued goods. If social order and stability are to be maintained, people should not have to deny each other the basic necessities of life.
>
> In many societies there is a sharp distinction between the way food and other goods are exchanged. If a society uses a form of money, it can often only be exchanged for socially valued 'wealth objects'. Frequently food cannot be bought or sold within the village or tribe: sometimes it is distributed equally between people and sometimes it is subject to some sort of gift exchange.
>
> Among the Siane of New Guinea there are three distinct groups of goods: The notion underlying the basis of distribution of food is that of equal shares, a balanced reciprocity. Luxury goods are exchanged according to self-interest in a nearly free market situation, and the exchange of ceremonial goods is a political affair accompanied by 'strict accounting'.[4,5]
>
> An important by-product of such systems concerns the homogeneity of societies. The more equitable the system for the distribution of food and other necessities, *the greater the identity of interest within the society when faced with ecological problems* [my italics].[6]

Wilkinson then contrasts these stable systems with the ecological imbalance of complex societies. However, it is not necessarily the complexity which is responsible for imbalance.[7] Human groups have been slowly expanding into new areas ever since they first left Africa less than 200,000 years ago. As the anthropological evidence drawn on by Wilkinson shows, some managed to return to an ecological equilibrium without destroying their environment. It would be useful for us to know how. As explained in the passage just quoted, we know that they eventually found a way of regulating their affairs sustainably, but not how they got back to that state after the luxury of not needing to.[8]

For most of the human race however, that process of slow expansion was still proceeding at the time of the Industrial Revolution in Europe. All those groups had spent countless millennia not obeying ecological constraints. They had not prevented their populations from slowly expanding, and even more important in highly developed societies, the development ethic was – is – deeply ingrained culturally as an alternative to population limitation. Wilkinson details the response of Europeans as they came up against the limits of their land to supply their needs. Expansion into colonies was a part of that response, but he points out that each of the innovations which constituted the Industrial Revolution had been just as feasible for several hundred years. If they were such a good idea, how come these changes did not happen until they were unavoidable?

The Polynesians were another group who had been able to continue expanding due to their seafaring ability. In most Polynesian societies population was traditionally stabilised by infanticide, abortion and coitus interruptus, though periodic inter-clan warfare reminiscent of chimpanzee communities was not unknown.[9] These avoided the much worse fate which befell the Easter Islanders. Many adventurous groups probably simply perished at sea. The overall pattern among Polynesian societies seems consistent with their having begun the transition back to sustainability, but not having had enough time to develop the comparatively conflict-free strategies found in New Guinea. Like Europeans, they were still prone to fall back on the aggressive 'default setting'. However, Easter Island was too remote to be in contact with anywhere else. It was large enough to let the group which discovered it forget traditional restraints for several hundred years, but too small to allow time to replace restraints when the exponential principle took them by surprise.

I have suggested that the world as a whole is on a similar course to ecological disaster. Fortunately, we have something the Easter Islanders lacked: not only their example, but also a model of societies which did make a successful transition back to stability. Most if not all have been changed out of recognition and incorporated into the global economy by now, but at least we know that there have been societies able to live within their means indefinitely. As the above quotation from *Poverty and Progress* makes clear, the Siane are only one example of many such societies.

Just as it would be a mistake to dismiss the Easter Islanders as more stupid than western global mankind, I am equally loath to assume that the Siane were more intelligent. With the advantage of the infrastructure and technology at our disposal which was not available to them, we should have no difficulty in instituting corresponding arrangements to abolish poverty *even as a possibility* at both a national and international level – once there is the recognition of the need, the political will, and a plan of how to do it.

Notes and References

1   Duane Elgin, *The 2020 Challenge*, Part 6. 'Two Scenarios: An evolutionary crash and bounce'. Internet website: www.newhorizons. org/ph_elgin2020f.html (as Chapter 2, Note 6)

2   Wilkinson, Richard G. (1973), *Poverty and Progress*, Methuen, London.

3   *Poverty and Progress* , p51.

4   Nash, Manning (1966), *Primitive and Peasant Economic Systems*, San Francisco pp. 48-51.
     Quoted in *Poverty and Progress*, p49.

5   Sahlins, Marshal D. (1965), 'On the sociology of primitive exchange', in Association of Social Anthropologists Monographs No 1, *The Relevance of Models in Social Anthropology*, pp139-236. Quoted in *Poverty and Progress,* p49.

6   *Poverty and Progress*, pp47-50.

7   I shall make clear in later Chapters that I am *not* advocating a 'deep Green' return to a primitive life-style.

8   See Descola, Philippe (1993), *The Spears of Twilight,* English translation (1996) HarperCollins, London for an account of life among the Jivaro in eastern Amazonia which was sustainable and free from inter-tribal warfare, but with a high level of vendetta related homicide. Bearing in mind that human colonization is believed to have been more recent in South America than in New Guinea, it is possible that this is an intermediate 'post-Tragedy' phase, before a more satisfactory sustainable culture has developed.

9   Firth, Raymond (1936) *We, The Tikopia*, Stanford U.P., Chapter XI, p374.

V

How it might happen

A paradigm for sustainability

The strategy for sustainability outlined in the quotation from *Poverty and Progress* in the last chapter can be set in a wider theoretical context. Imagine a globe with two opposite 'poles', lying on its side. This represents all possible resource sharing strategies. On the right is the 'ideal' that insists that each individual should fend for her or himself: no sharing whatsoever. There is an 'Arctic Circle' around this pole, which allows breadwinners to care for dependants. On the left is the ideal that all wealth should be shared equally and unconditionally among the community as a whole. Any strategy, theoretical or which has ever existed, can be plotted somewhere on this globe. It may attempt to accommodate the two extremes in a variety of ways, in which case it will be somewhere near the 'Equator', or it will be recognizably on one side, possibly paying some kind of lip service to the other.

This schema is confined to the issue of resource sharing, and is therefore simpler than 'right wing' and 'left wing' as generally understood. However, one other aspect of these two schools of thought which is obviously relevant to the discussion which follows is whether the family or the community should be the primary unit of individual support.

Consider what factors are likely to influence a society's choice of hemispheres, and what effect that choice might have on behaviour, either individually or collectively. The 'right wing', individualistic approach will put a premium on exploitation of opportunities, and so is well suited to take advantage where there is scope for expansion. However, it will deal harshly with anyone who fails to take advantage of opportunities, or who cannot, through no fault of their own. It will lead to conflict whenever those opportunities fail to materialise, and will therefore be prone to aggression, including racism when these conflicts become severe. It will create maximum pressure to exploit the environment without regard for the long-term consequences, because failure to exploit a genuine opportunity will have the same effect as the attempt to exploit one which is either bogus, or at best short term. It will be impossible to distinguish between bad luck, bad judgment or sheer idleness as the cause of destitution. These factors will render it permanently vulnerable to the Tragedy of the Commons.

'Left wing' egalitarianism on the other hand may well be the only way for a community to survive in harsh conditions, where resources are limited or unreliable. Clearly this 'pole' is the more consistent with ecological equilibrium. However, it would be expected to discourage, or at least fail to encourage innovation where it could be helpful. If the entire benefit is always to the community as a whole, none to the inventor or entrepreneur, that will obviously inhibit incentive. One would therefore expect egalitarian societies to be in harmony with their environment, internally happy and conflict-free, but needlessly impoverished by the standards of other societies, and certainly at a technological disadvantage, never having been under pressure to develop.

On this basis it comes as no surprise to find that the USA developed an aggressive right wing ethos during its formative years, and still clings firmly to it both domestically and in its foreign relations. The former communist countries were egalitarian in theory, but hardly so in practice, while there was in any case no popular consensus. Communism was imposed by Stalin everywhere in Europe except in Yugoslavia. My theory predicts that they should be environmentally friendly, and they were certainly not that. Nor was the flow of people desperate enough to get shot on the East German border evidence for the 'internal happiness' I anticipated.

I would argue that among the reasons why communist states both failed to live up to their ideals and ultimately failed economically was precisely because they had the wrong philosophy for the direction in which they were heading. They were trying to develop and expand their economies and compete with capitalism, not to aim for the stability and minimal demands on the environment to which a communal sharing strategy is suited. The space race notwithstanding, they did in most respects fall behind technologically. However, the current plight of many ex-communist countries is due more to outside influences than to the shortcomings of the old regime, a point I shall return to in later chapters. The only genuinely egalitarian societies of which I am aware were to be found in parts of the world untouched by western influences, such as Australia before the Europeans arrived.

Although the USA is a special case, one would expect any group, society or nation with perceived opportunities for expansion to favour a right rather than a left-wing strategy. As we have seen in earlier chapters, most groups of humans had been slowly expanding ever since their ancestors first left Africa, and for many that expansion has only very recently come up against serious limiting factors. Sometimes that expansion was imperceptible, but the important point is that just as the Siane had intuitively adopted a strategy appropriate to their circumstances as they perceived them, so these expanding groups had naturally enough done the same – in their case a strategy clearly in the 'right' hemisphere. When the time came to stop expanding, rather than change the basis of society, which had served at least the decision makers very well, they obviously tried to find new ways of developing. That led to innovations certainly, and there is no disputing the benefits of many of the fruits of development, even if it was the consequence of need rather than choice in the first place.

However, once expansion can no longer be relied on, a 'right hemisphere' strategy provides the conditions where poverty through maldistribution rather than actual shortage is to be expected. In fact this has been the norm rather than the exception ever since the introduction of permanent agriculture, despite the tremendous advances since then.[1] Arguably humankind first bumped its head 10,000 years ago against the ecological limits outlined in *Poverty and Progress*. Nevertheless the long era of gradual expansion continued. We saw in Chapter 3 that bonobos probably developed ways of defusing conflict because that was consistent with their settled environment, whilst chimpanzees are spasmodically aggressive towards neighbouring groups because that was more effective whilst they were extending their range – or experiencing Tragedies of the Commons. It is not surprising to find that different human groups have made similar choices.

It has been taken for granted in the Western world that the two polar opposites were mutually exclusive. But could there be ways of combining elements of each? I have suggested a 'globe' rather than a 'spectrum' to explain this concept because there are obviously any number of possible compromises. I shall return in Chapter 6 to the fact that Britain is one of many countries which have evolved surprisingly illogical and counterproductive compromises between pure self (or family) help and communal support. They have done so because they have no coherent strategy beyond the assumption that expansion will continue to be the norm. Where a society does not consider itself to have room for expansion, but nevertheless regards its environment as plentiful, then neither of the extremes is likely to be seen as appropriate. If there is an optimum combination the obvious place to look for it is among societies which have had the longest time for trial and error in a stable environment with plentiful, reliable resources. Which brings us back to the Siane.

The strategy adopted by the Siane and many other tribes in similar circumstances (at least until Europeans disturbed them) was to share basic necessities communally, but to allow a 'free market' in status goods. In other words, the 'left' pole for basic needs, and the 'right' pole for luxuries. Both socialism where it matters, and private enterprise where that is more useful; the best of both worlds. This gives a feeling of security to every member of that society, so that no one need feel under pressure to damage the environment out of desperation. For the same reason, there will be little or no reason for conflict over the things that really matter, only competition for things that don't when it comes to the crunch. But it also means that innovations and improvements can be rewarded. There must of course be a precondition that any changes must be demonstrably sustainable before they are let loose. This can easily be incorporated because there is not the pressure found in individualistic societies to develop regardless.

It must be noted that this strategy does assume and depend on a degree of wealth above basic subsistence. Only socialism – egalitarianism – will work without that. But above all, it is consistent with a steady-state economy, that is to say one which does not *depend* on economic growth. A Green economy does not mean zero economic activity. Zero economic *growth* may or may not turn out to be the norm, punctuated from time to time as environmentally sound innovations take effect, but the level of economic *activity* can be quite buoyant. We do not have to return to the Siane way of life, or to adopt any of their cultural patterns – only their basic strategy for sharing. Gaviotas demonstrates that a sustainable society can be extremely high-tech.

However, mention of Gaviotas brings me to another aspect of the potential reconciliation of 'right' and 'left'. As we learnt from Duane Elgin in the last chapter, although the Gaviotans have hit on one essential element – the automatic provision of necessities – they are recognizably socialist. Private enterprise would presumably be frowned on in a community where equal wages for all is the norm. It is not surprising that people from the left of the old political spectrum have found it easier to join the Green movement than those from the right. Social justice and a guarantee of security are absolute prerequisites for anyone expected to worry about the environment. In fact, many who are socialists as their first priority have joined the Green movement because they have realized that it offers a far stronger justification for egalitarianism than Marxism, locked in as Marx was to industrial development.

But people from all walks of life are capable of recognizing that we all depend on the biosphere for our continued existence. But those who dislike the provision of social security for people who fail to provide for themselves or fulfil their responsibilities, do have a conflict to resolve. They have to decide which is more important to them, everybody standing on their own two feet unaided, or caring for the environment, in which case they must concede the need to guarantee a feeling of security. Unfortunately existing Greens all too often tell would-be Green ex-Conservatives that only a socialist ethos can resolve this dilemma, so that the latter switch off and hope the problem will go away. These waters are muddied by the fact that most environmental ravages are perpetrated by rampant, aggressive multinational capitalists. This is taken as confirmation that socialism is environmentally sound (potentially true), whilst all private enterprise must be bad. (not true). Whether the most vicious dragons can be tamed or will have to be slain is not yet clear, but on both philosophical and practical grounds we ought to encourage as much small-scale private enterprise – and entrepreneurs – as is consistent with the overriding rule of sustainability, and the secondary rule of ensuring security for all.

The philosophical reason has already been mentioned. It is that innovators and entrepreneurs will have much to offer in terms of continued enhancement of the quality of life. Anything they come up with can be scrutinised, and taken on board if it satisfies the new rules. There will be no pressure either to accept or reject. If there is sufficient eco-friendly inventiveness, it may even be possible for economic growth to continue indefinitely. The practical reason is that if we are to have a hope in Hell of overcoming Scenario Two of the Tragedy of the Commons, we need every last one of these former natural Conservative sympathizers on our side.

So the strategy of ensuring security in basics, and encouraging initiative (or competition) for anything else, gives both sides of the old political divide most of what they want. Socialists may be disappointed that they have not after all vanquished their old enemies. But if the Siane knew no poverty, then with our resources and technology applied to this strategy we should be able to abolish it quite quickly. That was after all supposed to be the point of socialism. Smashing capitalism was only a means to that end.

Ex-Thatcherites on the other hand cannot tell people they must work or starve. They will have to accept a degree of redistribution. But everyone will be rewarded for whatever efforts they do make, and relatively large differences of status and wealth will still be possible – and reasonable.

Although I have suggested that it is easier for ex-socialists to embrace Green ideas than it is for ex-Conservatives, that is only true at the outset. In the longer term there are some dilemmas which socialists will find equally uncongenial. I shall discuss these in later chapters.

Once both sides have got their heads round this new concept – a sound union, a reconciliation of the two former polar opposites, not just an uneasy truce – we have the foundation for a new paradigm; a paradigm for sustainability. All we need then is a paradigm shift in its favour. A paradigm is something that everyone carries around in their head as an individual, but if enough millions of people share it, it must in due course become a force to be reckoned with. But we shall not replace Scenario Two with Scenario Three quite so easily. An expansionist ethos is deeply ingrained the world over. All that will happen next and into the foreseeable future is that instead of political struggles being primarily over how wealth should be shared, they will be between those who have confidence that human ingenuity will always find technological solutions to whatever problems we create for ourselves, and those of us who wish to usher in a new, sustainable phase in human history. We cannot even start this transformation until both sides of the old divide accept that their fight is out of date.

Reference

1   See Ponting, Clive (1991), *A Green History of the World*, Sinclair Stevenson, London, especially Chapters 4-7.

VI

Putting the theory into practice

The Citizens' Income

In the last two Chapters I have pointed out that tribes with minimal resources and rudimentary technology had no difficulty in sharing basic necessities and still having a surplus for status or other purposes without encroaching on their environment. The rest of this book is devoted to the proposition that what I shall call the Siane strategy can and must be adopted in the modern world both nationally and world-wide. A natural form for it to take at a national level in a complex Western state such as Britain or the United States is a Citizens' Income (CI). Similar schemes, called Basic Income, Social Dividend, Tax Credits or Negative Income Tax have been proposed for several years for a variety of reasons, and variation in detail reflects these different, indeed contradictory purposes.

The Citizens' Income is the principle that every man, woman and child should receive a weekly sum sufficient to cover the basic needs of food, fuel, clothing and accommodation. It will be tax free, paid to individuals and unconditional. So everyone will keep it whether they are working or not, or even whether they need it or not. The Citizens' Income will replace all existing social security benefits and income tax allowances for the able bodied. People on higher incomes could use it to offset tax liability instead of taking a cash payment. National insurance contributions, including for pensions will be subsumed into taxation.[1] In short, the CI is the unconditional provision of basic necessities for all from a common fund, provided by members of the community as a whole according to their ability to pay.

The basic concept is simple enough, but due to widespread misunderstanding of how this differs from the existing benefits system in a country such as Britain, most of this chapter is devoted to pointing out the unintended consequences of the latter. At present, a single person moving from Jobseeker's Allowance to a job loses so-called 'benefits' pound for pound. The CI will instead work like an extension of the present child benefit system. You need not work, but if you do, you keep your earnings, less tax. Under a means tested welfare support system basic necessities for those below the poverty line are in effect financed from the incomes of those only just above it. This admittedly startling claim can only be disputed by denying on principle the need for any support from outside the family, but as we saw in Chapter 5, that opinion is not open to anyone who believes in the need for sustainability. If society is to have an identity of interest in the face of ecological problems people must not deny each other basic necessities. For those on low pay, the loss of benefits as income from any other source becomes available is the same as though they were subject to punitive rates of tax. All the Citizens' Income does is shift this burden on to the shoulders of those higher up the income scale. Unfortunately, despite the self-evident social justice of a CI, this presents a formidable tactical reason why it has never been proposed by any political party hoping to be popular at the next election: the better off are more numerous – and more articulate – than the beneficiaries. Those who will have to pay for a CI will have to be persuaded, but first they must be convinced that means testing is indeed an oppressive tax in all but name.

I do not want to go into too much detail whilst explaining the basic principle underlying the Citizens' Income, but a few salient points will help. The weekly sum for adults will start at least at Jobseeker's Allowance or Income Support levels; i.e the minimum currently given out by the Benefits Agency, just over £53 per week in 2001-02. For the purely pragmatic reason that we want the large number of better off people who will pay more in tax than they receive from the Citizens' Income to give the idea a chance, the initial level of the Citizens' Income will have to be as low as possible. However these rates arguably do not reflect the basic needs of someone who may never have any other source of income, in which case they will have to be raised later, when the general public understands the new system.

The object of this strategy in the Green context is to give everyone a complete sense of security. It is redistributive, but its main purpose is to start a paradigm shift, or at least to make such a thing possible. To achieve anything at all it must be kept simple.[2] Even if the Green Party makes strenuous efforts to draw attention to the relevance of a Citizens' Income to ecological sustainability, for most people this first step towards a paradigm shift will be unwitting. It will be easier to adopt a less consumerist attitude, but that will not happen automatically. The point to keep clearly in mind throughout is that the Citizens' Income is no more than an appropriate way to implement the Siane strategy in a western democracy: sharing necessities, but sharing nothing else. To anyone coming to this topic 'cold', from a conventional standpoint, it must seem a bizarre idea. Workers paying for shirkers! It will cost billions, and we Greens propose to introduce it at the same time as we shut down all the sources of pollution that might conceivably pay for it.

As I hope to make clear, it is the present social security and tax arrangements which are bizarre. The Citizens' Income will have all kinds of consequences which I shall go into in the next few chapters, but my main purpose is to give millions of people a new idea to get their heads round. It will be just as dramatic as the change from believing the Earth is flat to believing that it is round, only with more immediate practical consequences. However, to illustrate my assertion that the present means tested benefits system is a disguised form of taxation on low incomes, I propose to approach the problem from an offbeat angle

It would be possible to introduce a Citizens' Income at the same level as Job seekers Allowance (JSA) in the next Budget. However, whilst this would indeed set in motion some much needed changes, to do so would cause some sharp discontinuities which would provoke hostility unnecessarily. Attempts to implement key Green policies will be severely hampered until a paradigm shift in people's thinking has taken place in sufficient numbers. Even this single proposal for a Citizens' Income at the lowest possible level will upset far more people than it pleases until they understand why. One possible way of starting the transition would be to introduce a Citizens' Income at JSA levels, but initially to put everyone back *through the tax system* into the same financial position as they are now, so that to begin with, no one would be affected at all. I must stress that the purpose of this charade is to change public perceptions of what is happening now, so that those on higher incomes who will pay more in taxation than they receive from a real Citizens' Income will understand why. It should never be necessary actually to implement a 'Zero effect' Citizens' Income.

This is how a 'Zero effect' CI would work: For simplicity, I will give the example of a single adult. Everyone, rich or poor, working or not, would receive and keep £53 per week (the JSA rate at the time of writing), regardless of any other considerations. However, at first, there would be a 100% tax rate on the first £53 per week that *everybody* received from other sources. That is of course an absolutely stupid way of doing things, but it

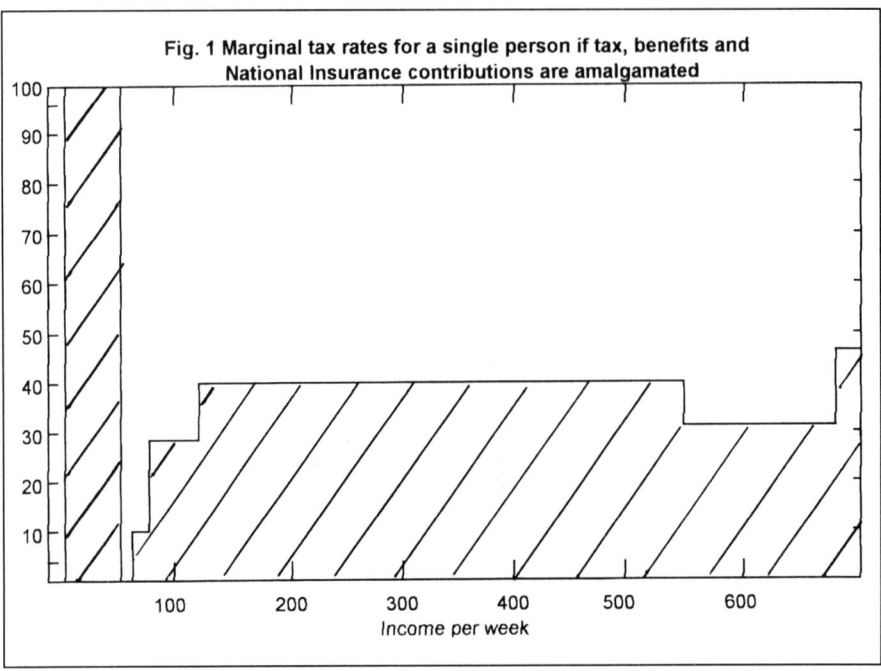

Fig. 1 Marginal tax rates for a single person if tax, benefits and National Insurance contributions are amalgamated

is what happens now. It is known as the poverty trap. What is at present done by not paying JSA to those who earn just a little too much to qualify, is for them effectively a disguised tax at 100%. The more affluent are also in the same position as if they had been given £53 per week, but were taxed at 100% on the first £2,756p.a. (£53x52) of their own earnings. The difference is that for them it is irrelevant. They have other money coming in. Most people are aware of the existence of the poverty trap, but do not realize that it has this effect.

A 'Zero effect' Citizens' Income is not suggested as a realistic way of introducing a true CI. One possibility would be a small, say £10 per week payment deducted from means tested payments. An 'employment bridge' payment will make sense to most people straight away. It is then a simple step to argue that the bridge should not sag, i.e. there should not be any level of income at which actual income drops. But it is necessary to get the '100% tax on low incomes' effect of what happens at present firmly fixed in people's minds so that they will understand why a true Citizens' Income makes sense, especially those who will have to pay for it. After all, tax, social security benefits and national insurance are all either payments to or by the government. What could be more logical than putting them together? So there would be no social security benefits or national insurance, just the Citizens' Income and taxes.

Table 1

Tax rates for a single person if the present tax, benefits and National Insurance payments are amalgamated (1999 Tax & NI rates)

Everyone would receive a sum equivalent to Income Support or Jobseekers Allowance, which they would keep in lieu of their personal tax allowance (which would be abolished).

Weekly Earnings (£)	Marginal Tax Rate (%)	New Tax Rate Replaces
0 – 5	0	Income support/ Jobseekers Allowance earnings disregard
6 – 56	100	Withdrawal of Income Support/JSA
57 – 66	0	Personal Allowance
67 – 83	10	Start of National Insurance
84 – 115	28.5	20% tax band + NI (Employee's *and* Employer's)
116 – 550	40.1	23% tax band + increased NI contribution
551 – 685	31.2	Employee's NIC ceases
686+	46.4	40% tax rate + Employer's NIC

I believe the fact that a means tested benefits system effectively creates a grotesque tax structure should be featured prominently by the Green Party at every election. Clearly a Citizens' Income will not initially be popular among the better off, and I shall discuss in Chapter 9 why only a Green Party dare broach this subject. But once people are aware of what the poverty trap actually does they will see all kinds of things in a different light. For example, moral outrage at 'working whilst claiming benefit' will look sanctimonious once that is recognized as the evasion of a preposterous 100% tax on the incomes of the lowest paid members of society. When recognition of this fact is commonplace, the way will be open to introduce a true Citizens' Income.

In order to firm up the explanation of how the poverty trap actually amounts to disguised but *real* taxes, Table 1 and Fig. 1 show what a 'transitional' tax structure (i.e. *not* the true CI) would look like for a single person over 25. In October 1999 the Chancellor of the Exchequer, Gordon Brown, introduced the Working Families Tax Credit (WFTC). This, and further tweakings in 2002 are actually small steps in the direction of a Citizens' Income, though they would not help the single person illustrated here. But it is an important part of my case that the CI is an idea which should be shouted from the house tops, not introduced surreptitiously. The figures I have used are not changing significantly from year to year, and they will still illustrate the principle when they are technically out of date

Table 1 and Fig. 1 show that there is a disguised tax rate of 100% on the lowest band of income, caused by the loss of Jobseekers Allowance. There is also a hump where people earning between £116 per week and £550 per week pay at a higher effective rate than those earning more due to national insurance deductions. Anyone on £120 per week loses a greater proportion of his/her income than someone earning five times as much. Table 1 and Fig. 1 show what is happening now, but under an amalgamated scheme of a Citizens' Income with idiotic tax rates, they would show actual tax deductions.

One point which is generally overlooked is that so far as an employer is concerned, both his/her and the employee's national insurance contributions are part of his/her wage bill, though the employee may not think of it as such. Take the example of a single person earning a gross wage of £200 per week. Their net pay under the present system would be £159 per week, calculated as follows:[3]

Example 1

Gross pay		200
Less employee's N I contribution	15	
Tax	26	41
Net pay		159

However, they also have 'unseen income' of £63 which has been deducted at source before they even knew they had it, as follows:

Example 2

Employer's N I contributions	14
Jobseeker's Allowance	49
	63

This becomes clear when you look at the same situation under the amalgamated CI and tax system. Now, workers keep their Jobseeker's Allowance (renamed Citizens' Income), thus putting everybody on the same starting line. Instead, they are taxed at 100% on an equivalent portion of their own earnings:

Example 3

Gross amount paid by employer	214
Less tax 15 + 26 + 14 + 49	104
Net wage	110
Citizens' Income	49
Total income	159

Proportion of earnings paid in tax (104÷214)   49%

If you do the same calculation for a gross wage of £300 per week, the proportion paid in tax falls to 46%, for a wage of £400 per week to 44%, and for £500 per week to 42%. This is shown in Fig. 2. At £100 per week, the proportion is 64%!

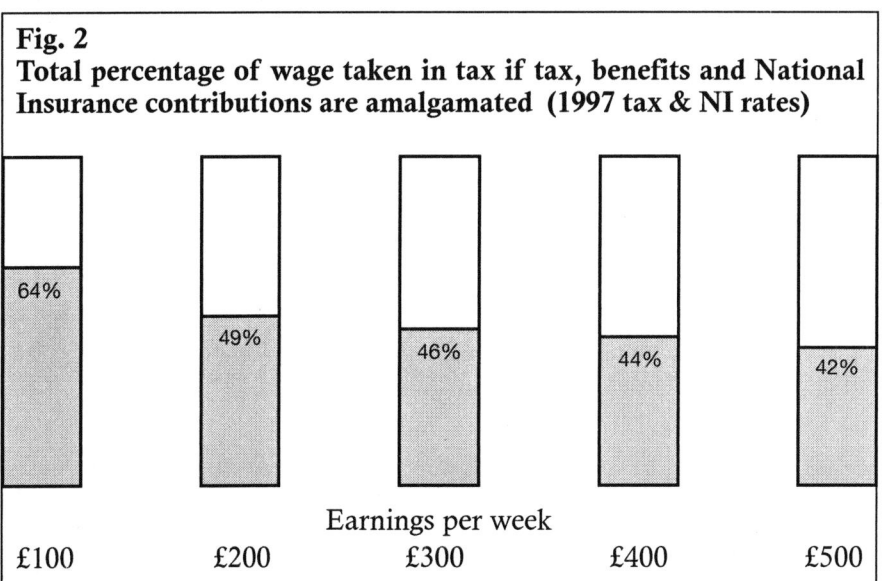

Fig. 2
Total percentage of wage taken in tax if tax, benefits and National Insurance contributions are amalgamated (1997 tax & NI rates)

64%

49%

46%

44%

42%

Earnings per week

£100   £200   £300   £400   £500

These figures and charts describe the simplest case of a single adult. Each different family situation would have to have its own set of tax rates. For example, a couple with children would have a tax rate of 55% on part of their income, to represent the rate at which Working Families Tax Credit is withdrawn per £ of increased earnings. A householder loses Housing Benefit (HB) at 65p in the £, so this too would have to be reproduced at the outset of a 'Zero effect' CI. The combined effect of 'targeting' WFTC and HB is to leave many families barely 10p better off from every pound they earn. So far as they are concerned, it might just as well take the form of a real tax at 90%.

Do please remember that this is not how a true Citizens' Income will work. It reproduces the present arrangements in a way which highlights just how silly and nasty they are. All governments since the Poor Law was first introduced in 1604 have fallen into this trap. To understand why we have to go back to the 'globe' I described in Chapter 5. Before 1604 we were simply in the 'no sharing' hemisphere, Henry VIII having abolished the monasteries which had alleviated poverty in previous centuries. The Poor Law/National Assistance/SupplementaryBenefits/Income Support/Jobseeker's Allowance, or whatever name it gets next, is a grudging acceptance that sheer destitution is inhumane, and it is not even in the interests of the rest of society. But because it is grudging, it is removed at the first opportunity. It was a first attempt to incorporate some element of the 'sharing' principle, but it is a peculiarly inept compromise. Without meaning to, it has the effect of saying 'Here is something to stave off starvation. By the way, if you do anything to help yourself, we will take it away from you'.

The effectiveness of the true Citizens' Income will be severely hampered until it is feasible to incorporate housing costs. I shall deal with this in more detail in Chapter 10, when I discuss transitional problems. Also, it may be necessary to defer the introduction of taxes designed to encourage Green trends and behaviour.

The cost

We have already seen that (a) the Citizens' Income is the expression of a tried and tested strategy – a community sharing unconditionally whatever is defined as necessary, but expecting either some contribution to society, or competition for anything else, and (b) the cost is being borne already – by the wrong people. Most people find this easier to grasp with the help of concrete figures.

A note on the historical context will help to explain how necessities are defined. From 1945 to 1979 there had been a tacit consensus between the Labour and Conservative parties on the social security arrangements. In 1979, when a Labour government gave way to 18 years of 'Thatcherite' Conservative rule, there were two Supplementary Benefit rates. The short term rate was the lower, for people who were assumed to be only temporarily without any other financial means. However, for a group of categories who were not expected to enter the labour market, or support themselves in any other way, there was the long term rate, which took the whole range of their needs into account. So until 1979 it was possible to use the long term rate as a definition of necessities.

However, the much more 'radical' government of Mrs Thatcher broke with that tradition, and steadily reduced the value of both long and short term rates. Finally in the late 1980s they scrapped the system and introduced a much tougher regime under which Income Support was even less than the short term rate had been. This is why I have already pointed out that the rate actually paid to people with no other entitlement may not in fact be sufficient to engender the feeling of security necessary for the next stage in my proposals.

The figures quoted in this book simply serve as a practical illustration of the underlying principle. Their usefulness is not limited to the financial year in which they were current. The relationship between the cost and the wealth available is not changing significantly from year to year. A few comments on Tables 2 and 3 may help to clarify them.

'Gross Domestic Product' (GDP) is the total income from all sources that every individual and every business declares to the Inland Revenue for tax purposes. Despite its weaknesses, GDP is more realistic than personal disposable income as a measure of the total spending power sloshing around the country. However, since it is what people, firms or their accountants actually admit to, it is almost certainly an underestimate. As Green ideals are put into practice and the economy becomes more informal, GDP may become less useful as a guide. But as has already been noted, a Green economy does not mean no economic activity, just a vibrant, sustainable economy where growth can no longer be taken for granted.

One criticism sometimes heard is that Green policies will erode their own tax base. But unless an economy has been so abused that it cannot even produce enough to provide basic necessities for its citizens, there will always be enough wealth circulating, or economic activity whose proceeds can be shared for this purpose. The Citizens' Income, taxation, and specifically income tax, are merely the simplest means to that end at the outset. As Table 3 shows, the ratio of GDP to the gross cost of the Citizens'

Table 2
Citizens' Income costings (1999-2000 figures)[9]

Age		£ billion per annum
0 – 11	8.5 million @ £20.20 p.w.	8.93
11 – 16	4.5 million @ £25.90 p.w.	6.06
16 – 19	2.7 million @ £30.95 p.w.	4.35
20 – 60	30.2 million @ £52.20 p.w.	81.97
60+	12 million @ £75.00 -p.w.	46.8
Disability Supplement	2 million @ £25.00 p.w.	2.6
Accommodation Allowance[1]	46 million @ £22.00 p.w.	52.62

Gross cost of Citizens' Income		**203.33**

Payments which would cease

Social Security payments[2]			93.81
Housing Benefit and subsidies[2]			3.77
Tax Allowances			
Starting Rate	£4385 x 1 million x 10%	0.44	
	£2000 x 0.5 million x 10%	0.1	
Basic Rate	£4385 x 22 million x 22%	21.22	
	£2000 x 8 million x 22%	3.52	
Higher Rate	£4385 x 2 million x 40%	3.51	
	£2000 x 1 million x 40%	0.8	
Administration costs saved		4.35	
Less savings			**131.52**
Net cost			**71.81**

<u>**Notes**</u>
1. The accommodation component of the Citizens' Income will be complicated to introduce. Eventually it will be given in full to every individual, calculated according to rents separately in each Local Authority area. Initially it will only be given in full to single householders. Other households will receive a partial allowance.
The figure given is an estimate of an initial transitional figure averaged out over the whole population. £22 p.w. is not the amount to be received by those still in need.[10]
2. Office for National Statistics Annual Abstract of Statistics 2000

Table 3
Cost of the Citizens' Income in relation to Gross Domestic Product

Gross Domestic Product[9]	**£773.38 bn per annum**
Gross cost of Citizens' Income	**26.3% of GDP**
Net cost	**9.3% of GDP**

(From figures in Table 2)

Income is about 3:1. The net cost, after deducting the value of benefits and tax allowances which will be abolished, is 10% of GDP.

It has been estimated that a Citizens' Income for adults at Jobseeker's Allowance levels could be implemented with a flat rate of income tax of 29%.[4] Presumably one reason the Chancellor of the Exchequer feels the need to be surreptitious about moves in this direction (if indeed he is moving that way wittingly) is that he thinks this would be unpopular. Without a coherent philosophy to justify it, he may be right. But turn back for a moment to Fig. 1 – showing the tax structure as it really is now. That extra 7%, or 29p in the £ instead of 22p, is all it would take to remove the poverty trap; to change the crazy graph illustrated in Fig. 1 to a straight line right across; to move from the present self-defeating grudging arrangements to a strategy of sharing basic needs unconditionally. I cannot repeat too often that the 'cost' is being paid already by those working on low incomes, in the form of loss of 'benefits'.

It will, as I have mentioned, 'cost' more to bring the Citizens' Income back up to the level corresponding to the 1979 long term supplementary benefits rate. It must not be forgotten that Jobseeker's Allowance rates are deliberately intended *not* to allow recipients to feel secure, and the Labour government since 1997 has not seen fit to change that. But the correct rate is a debate which can take place when we have laid the foundations of this completely new approach. Old political differences of opinion will not disappear completely. Some will argue that a Citizens' Income should be based on the family, others on individuals. Another discussion will be whether it should be relatively high, with everyone responsible for their own health, education, transport, dustbins etc., or lower with most services free or at a nominal cost, as in Gaviotas. But instead of these being the major bones of contention, the CI will allow them to become subsidiary to the crucial debate between conservationists and expansionists.

As to how the money should be raised, I have assumed throughout this explanation that income tax would be the vehicle, even when the true Citizens' Income is in operation. It is fair; it is the only method which allows a direct 'before and after' comparison; its effect is predictable; and rates can be changed quickly if expectations prove inaccurate.

There is however a school of thought within the Green movement that income tax and VAT harm incentives without helping environmental considerations, and should therefore be phased out in favour of resource taxes.[5] This is a discussion which would be better postponed. To the extent that resource taxes will increase the cost of basic necessities, the Citizens' Income will have to be raised to cover that increase. Getting the Citizens' Income message across will be a hard enough task kept to its simplest and least disturbing to the 'haves'. My Green Party colleague Jonathan Dixon has offered an ingenious answer to the problem of 'selling' the Citizens' Income.[6] Instead of paying it in cash, present it as a Tax Credit, refundable in cash if not used up against income. That way both income tax and the social security bill will appear to be reduced, yet people will be in exactly the same position as they would have been with a Citizens' Income, because that is what it really is.

There are other possible ways of funding the Citizens' Income. The one way which will *not* normally be available is deficit financing. In 1974, Sir Keith Joseph, a leading member of the then Conservative government, proposed a Tax Credit scheme not backed by taxation, with the intention of promoting economic growth! It would have worked like the rule in the game of Monopoly 'Collect £200 every time you pass Go' The versatility of the Citizens' Income is such that it could be used for quite the opposite of emulating the Siane! However, if the economy was for any reason performing at a lower level than ecological considerations would permit, to pay out the Citizens' Income temporarily without fully balancing it with equivalent taxation could be a way to correct that.

VAT, unlike income tax, could go beyond 100%, so that the rich could choose for themselves how and when to pay, as tax would only be payable on spending.[7] But like income tax, VAT inhibits economic activity without benefiting the environment. It also aggravates fluctuations in the price of goods. Energy taxes could be based on the calorific value of each fuel, and could be varied according to its sustainability or environmental impact. Non-renewable resources can be taxed at the point of extraction. However, taxes intended primarily to reduce environmental degradation cannot at the same time be relied on for revenue in the long term. One resource which cannot be either increased or reduced is land, so a Land Value Tax[8] may become important as other means of guaranteeing basic needs through the tax system become less feasible.

However, as explained, all these options would be better kept out of the debate until the principle is generally understood, namely that if a society is serious about living sustainably, then it must guarantee every citizen basic needs as of right. In practice, in Britain, that means giving everyone at least £55 per week (less for children), no questions asked, and paying for it by raising the standard rate of income tax.

Notes and References

1   Health and/or unemployment insurance would be a personal matter, though an optional national scheme could be retained. Supplements for disability are a separate issue, not considered here.

2   Some advocates of a Citizens' Income suggest a once in a lifetime capital payment in preference to periodic payments. A paper on this topic was presented by Bernard Berteloot to the 8th Congress of the Basic Income European Network (BIEN) in Berlin, 6/7 October, 2000.

3   The figures used are taken from an unpublished paper by Jonathan Dixon, of Scarborough Green Party. They are based on 1997 tax and National Insurance rates, but the principle illustrated will continue to apply until a Citizens' Income is introduced.

4   Extrapolated from Desai, M (1998), 'A Basic Income Proposal', *The State of the Future,* Social Market Foundation, London. The 29% rate (compared to a standard rate of 22% at the time of writing) assumes that National Insurance is retained and extended to cover all incomes, and that higher rate tax is also increased by 7%.

An OECD study estimated that a Basic Income plan that paid a benefit of 30% of the average personal factor income would require a tax rate of 39.3% for the United States, 34.5% for Australia, 35.6% for France, and 37.5% for the United Kingdom. Clark, Charles M.A and Kavanagh, Catherine (June 1996): 'Basic income, inequality, and unemployment: rethinking the linkage between work and welfare', *Journal of Economic Issues,* v30 n2, p399(8).

5   Robertson, James (1999), *The New Economics of Sustainable Development: A Briefing for Policy Makers,* Kogan Page, London.

6   Based on a further unpublished paper by Jonathan Dixon.

7   At the time of writing, Green Party policy is to abolish VAT.

8   I.e. a tax on the unimproved rental value of land.

9   Figures based on Office for National Statistics, *Annual Abstract of Statistics 2000.*

10   The full introduction of the Accommodation Allowance is discussed in Chapter 10. Transitionally, everyone who receives means-tested support will continue to do so at the same rate.

VII

The effect of the Citizens' Income

(i) Practical effects

One of the most immediate, and immediately obvious advantages of a real Citizens' Income – an unconditional payment to every individual, rich or poor, working or not – will be its effect on employment, and the relationship between employment and the jobs which society needs doing. It combines a guarantee of security with a previously missing work *incentive*. So there is no need for compulsion. For anyone who does choose not to work for a wage, the effective contract between them and the rest of society is 'I guarantee to take no more from the economy than is necessary for my subsistence'. They will always be materially worse off than everybody else, unless of course they have income other than from employment. Such people have never been compelled to work.

One consequence of the introduction of a Citizens' Income is that some parts of the 'Black Economy' can become honest and join the 'Green Economy'. Tax evasion is likely to be less prevalent than claiming benefit whilst working is now. It is worth risking prosecution if 100% or even 70% of your earnings is at stake, but less so if you only have to pay around one third in tax.

There has always been something illogical about insisting that everyone should have to work as long as there is any unemployment whatsoever. Yet on the other hand, the Citizens' Income also means that for the first time work can be made available for all who want it. The very concept of unemployment can be consigned to the history books. Paid work can be anything from a few minutes to 80 or more hours per week. This new flexibility will have less immediate relevance to people already on the higher rungs of the income ladder, with a family and mortgage. However it will allow more flexibility in career choices and moves, and it will cushion the savage blow felt by anyone who is unexpectedly made redundant from a well paid and supposedly secure post. It will also open up more options for the unemployed, and those for whom unemployment is a real threat, or in and out of casual work, at present continually harassed by officialdom to take a totally unsuitable job or else.

For the low paid, a new millennium really will have arrived. Take the example of a family man with a wife and 2 children, working 40 hours per week at a minimum wage of £3.60 per hour. Suppose that his wife works 20 hours at the same rate. They qualify for Working Families Tax Credit (WFTC), which as we have seen, is a short step in the right direction. However, for the sake of simplicity, I am assuming that support for children will be at least equivalent to their current entitlement to WFTC.[1] The family's income before the change is £3.60 x 60 hours = £216.00 per week gross. £49 is taken in tax and National Insurance, so their combined net wages are £167. With a Citizens' Income of £52 per week, they would gain £104 per week between them but with a probable tax rate of 43% (absorbing National Insurance contributions) on all their earnings they would pay £44 more in tax. So their net gain would be £60 per week -a 36% pay rise!

But complete flexibility in job availability does however entail corresponding flexibility in wage rates. These too can vary along a continuum from the kind of completely voluntary jobs traditionally undertaken by the Vicar's wife, through semi voluntary work which carries some sort of honorarium, via more substantial hourly rates up to the kind of rewards expected by Premier League footballers. On the one hand, ridiculously astronomical incomes do not matter as long as the environment is not harmed, and no one is going without basic needs. But on the other hand, whatever is earned is a top up in addition to the Citizens' Income. Any earnings are by definition over and above subsistence needs.

Consider the following two propositions:

(1) All jobs which need doing should get done at a price society can afford; and

(2) Everyone who wants paid work should have the opportunity to find it.

On this basis, it does not matter who does the work, or even whether people do it at all, so long as the goods or services are provided. But many potential jobs in a conservation based economy will only be feasible if they can be low paid: recycling materials, weeding instead of using pesticides on organic farms, many kinds of repair work to prevent the wasteful use of resources. Whether these and many other labour intensive environmentally friendly jobs are feasible at all will depend on how low the hourly rate can be. Yet far from being exploitative, the CI sets up a genuinely free market, where the potential employee has bargaining power no Trade Union was ever able to give her/him. Everyone can make an individual decision whether to take a job at the hourly rate offered. Too low, and he/she can stay at home. A study done in the Netherlands in 1995[2] expressed the fear that although the overall effects of a Citizens' Income were likely to be beneficial, one of its drawbacks as the authors saw it, was that the hourly rate for unpleasant jobs might rise too high! In the opinion of Trade Unionists I have spoken to over the years, on balance hourly wage rates would go down rather than up under a CI, but they overlook the potential for large numbers of additional low paid jobs.

It will not have escaped the reader's notice that the foregoing conflicts with the principle of a minimum wage. That becomes unnecessary because the Citizens' Income does what a minimum wage is supposed to do, but without its potential drawbacks of inhibiting job availability and fuelling demands to restore differentials. However, the minimum wage does not just militate against the potential benefits of a Citizens' Income, it is incompatible with a sustainable economy. If it is set low, it does not guarantee a sufficient income anyway. If it is set high, the arguments by Conservatives that it will price useful jobs out of the market and aggravate inflation must be true *unless the economy goes on expanding*. As long as a living income is tied to jobs, then jobs will have to be created regardless of the consequences, environmental or otherwise. A minimum wage would ruin the flexibility and potential for job creation which the Citizens' Income offers.

Perhaps the clearest illustration of wage rate flexibility allowed by the Citizens' Income is that of a self-employed person. At present he or she only breaks even when profits reach Unemployment Benefit levels, slightly higher than the Jobseeker's Allowance. As a top-up to the CI, a business is viable as long as it makes any money at all. Some would-be entrepreneurs may even be able to carry losses for a period. This will allow anyone with a business idea to 'go for it'. Provided it is environmentally sound, there is no harm done if it succeeds, and no serious harm done if he/she has to fall back on the Citizens' Income. The same applies to any budding artist or musician. You want to go back to education, or train for something different in your mid-forties? No need to apply for a grant. Similarly, anyone who wants to try complete self-sufficiency on an abandoned Hebridean croft – good luck to them. If they reach the point where they no longer need their CI, they can donate it to the charity of their choice if they don't want a few little luxuries.

The Citizens' Income will act like a piggy-bank for any small business prone to a wildly fluctuating income. Farmers are a typical example of this. In good times they will be net payers, but when prices hit rock-bottom, the CI will be a lifeline. To take things a step further, suppose a one-person business, a plumber say, reaches the point where due to recommendations by satisfied customers he can't quite keep up with the flow of orders. He would like to take on a school-leaver part-time. He cannot afford to pay a high wage, and in any case he wants to see how the lad (or lass) shapes up before committing himself. If all goes well, business will continue to grow organically, and the trainee if satisfactory will become a full time apprentice. Her/his worth will however still be limited by inexperience, but here again, a relatively low wage will be topping up the Citizens' Income to a level at least as high as a minimum wage would be likely to reach.

These examples will be quietly repeated a million fold, to the mutual benefit of both employer and potential recruit. Widespread criticisms of the artificial 'Job Creation' attempted in Britain during the 1980s and 90s. were often unfair, but they were arbitrary, and the schemes were discontinued. The Citizens' Income will achieve the same but more spontaneously and on a permanent basis. One of the criticisms levelled at a Citizens' Income is that it 'subsidises employers'. Of course it does! If the labour-intensive jobs that are part and parcel of a sustainable economy are to be feasible, they will have to be 'subsidised' somehow.[3] But that is not a helpful way of viewing the Citizens' Income. It betrays an attitude that is more concerned with penalizing old enemies than rescuing unemployed allies. Any other way of subsidizing employment would have to be bureaucratic by comparison, inefficient and prone to loopholes which could be abused.

Another spontaneous development which will become feasible is people in time-demanding jobs paying people who would otherwise be unemployed to do their gardening, cleaning, nannying, or whatever they have too little time and too much stress to do. Of course this is done already by single professionals and in well to do circles, but here again, the wage rate and time flexibility made possible by the Citizens' Income will open it up to a much wider circle of potential employers and the otherwise unemployed. There are many Local Authority jobs which could benefit from a pool of available casual low paid workers. Not that it happens much in practice in Britain nowadays due to global warming, but the speedy removal of a heavy snowfall on streets which would otherwise be left unattended would be an example of this. In all these examples, the 'free market' of choice by the unemployed whether this or that job offer was worth their while would operate. Part time and casual work are already more widespread in Britain than elsewhere, but the poverty trap still rules it out for the main family breadwinner.

Single parents, or anyone for that matter with limited or variable time available, will find countless new opportunities for topping up their Citizens' Income. This opens up a whole new area where the CI has an unexpected beneficial effect. The laudable purpose of the Child Support Agency is to hold absent parents to account for financial responsibilities they have created. Surprise surprise, it hit the same snag which has always bedevilled the Poor Law and its successors. It has proved difficult if not impossible to determine who could pay, and who genuinely cannot. The system has vacillated from complex to simple and arbitrary, most of the time leaving both caring and absent parent aggrieved. A major part of the problem stems, as always, directly from the social security generated poverty trap. If an absent parent is earning, he can be clobbered. If he is unemployed, the Benefits Agency has to pick up the bill for his child maintenance. So every absent parent is under pressure to choose the latter option. With a Citizens' Income, a proportion of any earnings can be deducted, leaving the absent parent still better off working.

Looking at the effect of a Citizens' Income from the 'macro' point of view, we used to hear how automation was going to create a Leisure Society. With the need to prevent unemployment removed, where machines can do the job as well if not better without people interfering, there is no reason not to let them get on with it. The general pattern, which I hope is emerging, is that the Citizens' Income will encourage as vibrant an economy as is consistent with the ecological ceiling.

Nevertheless a sustainable economy will have to do without apparently soft options which the public still takes for granted. I shall return later to the principle that Green economics may involve replacing economic growth as an aim with that of a steady state economy. But from a conventional standpoint the latter is likely to resemble a permanent if mild recession by historical standards, with the restricted options which that entails. Even worse, if the transition is uneven, there could be many business casualties, some of which may well be ecologically innocent. Conventional economic pundits tell us that demand must be kept up or we shall fall into a self-perpetuating recession with bankruptcies creating a 'domino' effect. We must keep buying things whether we need them or not, and regardless of poverty elsewhere. Whilst one can follow the reasoning, it does look like arrant nonsense when one bears in mind that the Siane combined sustainability and security with a competitive free market in luxury goods. With our technological advantages, a steady state economy ought to be at least as easy for us to achieve – and maintain – as it was for them.

The Citizens' Income will dampen down economic oscillations and ensure that a certain amount of money is always flowing through the system. In the last chapter I admitted that higher taxation is inevitable, and this will help to inhibit booms. On the other hand in his book *The Ecology of Money*, Richard Douthwaite points out that a significant reason why a slump on the scale of 1929 has not happened in Western Europe since the Second World War is social security payments. They are spent back into the economy immediately, regardless of the economic climate.[4] The Citizens' Income consolidates this mechanism and removes the instability inherent in a system where funding dries up just when the need for payouts is at its greatest. Economic instability can be further dampened down by raising or lowering taxation. I shall return in the next chapter to the possibility that the CI could in time create an atmosphere where the pressure for consumer durables and for economic growth generally can be reduced, and hence bring about the changes in attitudes necessary if any of this is to become feasible.

A somewhat complex area which must be covered by the Citizens' Income when it is fully operational is housing and accommodation generally. Whereas uniform national rates are envisaged for the other basic necessities of food, fuel and clothing, accommodation will presumably have to be determined locally, due to the wild disparity in the cost of accommodation across Britain. The ultimate aim, as with other necessities, is to remove the poverty trap: to give everyone from the tramp in a cardboard box to the rich man in his castle an amount which will cover standard accommodation needs, and to balance it with taxation from the sections of society best able to afford it. This problem is rendered even more difficult to disentangle by distortions in the housing market, due largely to well meaning, but partial and incoherent attempts to fix particular aspects.

One such distortion which the Citizens' Income will correct is due to the fact that couples get less social security than two individuals. The 'cohabitation rule' means that couples who actually get on well together, and would like to bring up their children together, are forced to pretend, or actually to live apart. The Conservative party, which prides itself on family values, saw nothing wrong with this

The accommodation component of a Citizens' Income will need a lengthy phasing in period, whilst the anomalies are sorted out. Also, the sums involved will be quite large. Eventually it should be possible to give each man, woman and child a fixed sum, standard within a given Local Authority area. One major effect will be that everybody will get it. At present, those who need it most, those who live in cardboard boxes, get nothing *because* they have no accommodation. The long-term benefit will be that once a genuinely free market exists – with would-be tenants, like casual workers, given something to bargain with – that market will begin to cater for actual demand. But it will take years to take full effect. If someone hardened to the rigours of life on the streets chose to spend his accommodation allowance on drink, that would be his business. Anyone who wanted to get back into accommodation as quickly as possible could save up their allowance.[5]

This seems a good point to mention begging. It was no coincidence that begging as a serious phenomenon reappeared in the course of the Conservative government's measures to crack down on scroungers in the 1980s. With a Citizens' Income, anyone who did beg would simply not be believed.

In September 1988 I attended a Basic Income European Network (BIEN) Conference in Antwerp, which was addressed by Chris O'Malley, then a Fine Gael (Irish) Member of the European Parliament (MEP). He pointed out that the Basic Income (as the CI was then generally referred to) would actually serve his constituents on marginal hill farms far better than the Common Agricultural Policy (CAP). These arrangements are specifically intended to protect small European farmers, but do so in a way which has unintended side-effects for everyone else.[6] The cost of the CAP could be deducted from the net cost of the CI. As we have seen, the CI has the additional advantage of damping down fluctuations in farm incomes.

With the onset of insecurity during the 1990s, strikes have become rare by the standards of 25 years ago. With the Citizens' Income to fall back on, it will be easier to strike on matters of principle, such as health and safety issues. However, the loss to the striker will be his/her whole wage. For a single person with no dependants, that is the situation now, but if a striker has dependants, they are given Income Support, so for him/her the calculation is loss of his wages *minus* social security payments to his/her family. So the introduction of a CI will make strikes over pay less likely.

(ii) Some common questions answered

The answers to most of the following questions should be emerging from the story so far, but it may nevertheless help to deal with them specifically.

'Doesn't a Citizens' Income mean workers paying for shirkers?'

This is the most frequently asked question apart from the cost, which was covered in the last chapter. The short answer is no, quite the opposite. Anyone who phrases the question in that way, and a depressing number do, has presumably not experienced the poverty trap at first hand. Due to the real but disguised tax rates explained in the last chapter, those in *low paid* employment have been paying for those who were out of work ever since the Poor Law introduced by Queen Elizabeth I gave not working an advantage over working at low pay. This applies even if the unemployed have tried desperately to find work. Over the years there have been attempts to define 'deserving' and 'undeserving' poor, There have been lax periods, such as the Speenhamland system after 1795, and periodic tightenings of the rules, for example the Poor Law of 1834. It was never satisfactory. These vacillations reflected the fact that it was and always will be impossible to define 'deserving' in practice.

The 'Beveridge' Report in 1945 attempted to resolve this dilemma by introducing a comprehensive National Insurance based welfare state. This would rely on full employment, but the Labour government which implemented the report was in any case determined that full employment was to be a permanent state of affairs. However just in case, as full employment had never been achieved in the past even for brief periods, they had to include 'National Assistance', which would be paid to anyone who was destitute and was not entitled to any other source of income, even if they had never worked or paid contributions. Like the Poor Law before it, National Assistance would be given on condition the recipient did not work. That was not the intention of course, but its effect was to pull the rug from under anyone who really was destitute if they did anything to help themselves. Lady Rhys Williams, a prominent Liberal on the Beveridge Commission, produced a minority report pointing out this weakness, and proposing a Basic (i.e. Citizens') Income. The Trade Union members of the Commission even suppressed publication of Lady Rhys Williams' report, insisting that social security must be based on male, full time breadwinners.

The 'Beveridge' plan was an improvement on the piecemeal arrangements it replaced, but despite three and a half centuries of experience to the contrary, it was hoped that this serious structural flaw could be ignored – except by those caught in the poverty trap which it creates – because full employment was going to be the norm from then on. This myth could only be sustained as long as full employment seemed a realistic goal.

However, as unemployment soared past the million mark in 1979, and rose to 3 million in the mid 1980s, 'handouts' of Supplementary Benefits as they were now called became a serious problem. The social security bill rocketed. Between 1979 and 1997 the Conservative government repeated the history of 1834. One forms the impression that Mrs. Thatcher would have liked to abolish welfare benefits altogether, being personally close to the 'right wing' pole described in Chapter 5. The government settled for a succession of reductions in benefits and tightenings of the rules of entitlement, which proved just as difficult to interpret as the Poor Law. The Labour government in power since 1997 did not reverse those 'reforms'. Despite minor moves in the direction of a Citizens' Income made by the Chancellor of the Exchequer, the low paid are still paying for the unemployed, and they understandably resent it.

With a Citizens' Income there is no obligation to work, but anyone who does is better off than anyone who does not. That is not so at present. The converse is that those on the lowest incomes are at last better off in work, even low paid work, than 'on the dole'. If there is such a thing as a shirker, he has been encouraged by the arrangements for the relief of poverty ever since 1604. Anyone who insists on it can still think of themselves as workers paying for shirkers, but the Citizens' Income brings to an end the incentive to rely on handouts. It certainly does not create it.

Nevertheless many people feel unease at no longer enforcing the work ethic. They are worried that large numbers will simply down tools and happily accept release from drudgery. In any case, they still feel that everybody ought to have to contribute to society in this way. In the first place, people who could avoid 'work' due to having private means would still be exempt. Once again I must repeat, the Citizens' Income actually reinstates a work incentive which has been obstructed by the poverty trap for 400 years. It is illogical to fear that people will down tools. Anyone who does will have to accept a subsistence standard of living. Many people work without being financially better off for all kinds of reasons. A more realistic worry from a Green perspective is that too many will continue to be consumerist. Whichever happens in practice can be corrected by raising or lowering taxation. It is part of my theme that excess consumerism is driving us on to the rocks. I believe its momentum is such that it is unlikely to disappear quite so suddenly.

The forms which alternatives to a Citizens' Income could take are limited. Conditional relief could be extended, either in scope (including categories) or amount, but this would simply make the poverty trap bigger. The only other direction for reform that I can envisage would be further *reductions* in social security. This would be the right wing solution, with all the disadvantages outlined in Chapter 5. Anyone who thinks that is remotely feasible is not only impervious to the suffering of the countless innocent victims there would be, but is not furthering their own long term interests. Life would become increasingly insecure at all levels. The rich would pay far more than they would gain in lower taxes, just to fortify and insure their residences. The majority would simply live in fear of those more desperate than themselves, and agonize over whether to pay astronomical insurance premiums in the meantime.

Above all reducing social security would rule out any possibility of seeking to live sustainably within the Earth's resources, as it would put a premium on economic expansion at all costs. There is a strand in the Green movement which believes that self-reliance should be an important element in a Green, sustainable society. It will certainly help if people can be taught to be self-reliant without conflicting with the absolute precondition of a complete sense of security – for everyone. No doubt much can and will be done to make sustainable self-reliance a reality, but for millions world-wide, it is simply not a realistic option in the short term.

There is a philosophical justification for voluntary work incentives rather than coercion.[7] The work ethic and the conservation ethic can be regarded as opposite sides of the same coin. In an expanding society exploiting new resources, the work ethic is vital, especially before technology can take some of the strain. The conservation ethic is morally right, but not essential. There is plenty more where that came from provided you work hard. But we are now in a situation where we need to conserve what we have acquired, where we must husband finite resources, and where it is increasingly difficult to find somewhere to put toxic rubbish. So now it is the conservation ethic which is important. The work ethic remains 'morally right' but becomes superfluous, especially when machines now do so much of the work. Waste is the crime rather than idleness.

To insist that the CI should be conditional on work would simply not be doing what the Siane have demonstrated works. Those who think along these lines tend also to suggest a 'cut off' point above which people who do not need the Citizens' Income should not receive it. This misunderstands the whole principle involved. A 'cut off' point anywhere re-creates

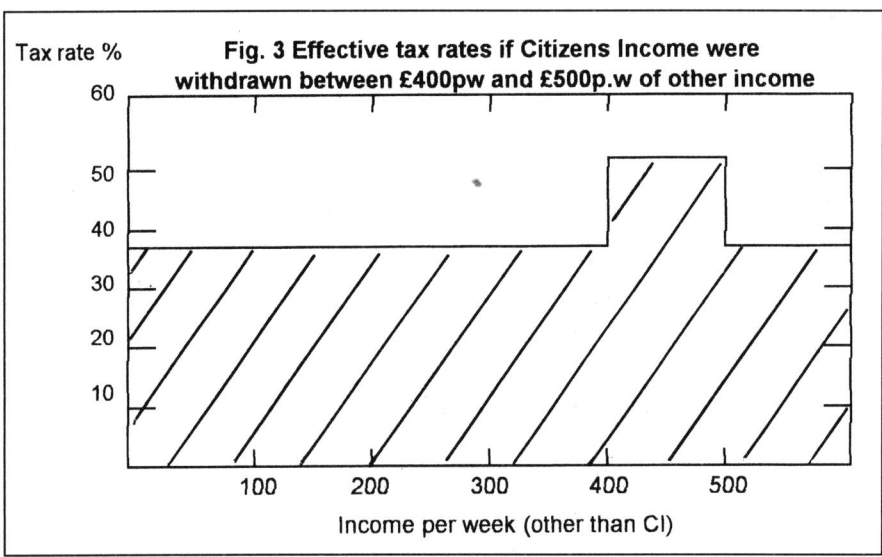

Fig. 3 Effective tax rates if Citizens Income were withdrawn between £400pw and £500p.w of other income

the illogical tax structure depicted in Table 1 and Fig. 1 in the last chapter. Suppose for example that a CI of £52 is withdrawn at £400p.w., and the tax rate is 37%. A, earning £399p.w. has a total of £52+£399–£147(tax)=£304. B, on £401p.w. receives £401–£148=£253. That would be clearly unacceptable. If you try to soften the blow with a 'taper' – withdrawing the CI at any rate higher than 37 pence in the pound of earnings above £400, like Family Credit now, you just re-create the kind of 'hump' seen in Fig. 1, Chapter 6. If it were withdrawn at 52 pence in the £, so that the CI was completely withdrawn between £400p.w. and £500p.w., the effective tax structure would look like Fig.3. We get away with it without too much fuss because this arbitrary injustice is currently perpetrated on the most demoralized inarticulate and disorganized sections of society. I shudder to think what would happen if it were visited on a section of the middle classes.

'Won't a Citizens' Income drive wages down?'

Trade Unionists have tended to dislike the Citizens' Income because it would erode their power base. 'Driving wages down' is of course a variation on the 'subsidizing employers' theme, to which I have already pleaded guilty. But what matters to an employee is total income, not who pays it. The employee *will* quite rightly down tools if he judges that the unpleasant game he has hitherto been forced to play is not worth the candle. In that case wages will be driven up, as the Dutch study mentioned earlier suggests.[2] So a better way of expressing this point is that the CI allows wages to find a level that is mutually beneficial to entrepreneurs, employees and a sustainable economy. There is an example which might help to illustrate this point. During a strike by ambulance drivers, they pointed out that there were more resignations than new recruits coming forward, demonstrating that their pay was too low. That yardstick could become a regular component of wage negotiations.

'Capitalists will never allow such a redistributive measure.'

This is class warfare in yet another guise. As long as avowed socialists, whether revolutionary or democratic, let it be known that they will dismantle the capitalist system as soon as they are strong enough, they must not be surprised if capitalists use their existing power to ensure that they never are. But with a Citizens' Income, not only can the capitalists keep a lot of the gravy, but sustainability offers the prospect of the bounty lasting rather longer than it otherwise would. Just as low paid workers have less incentive to hide their earnings if they can keep most of them, so there is less incentive to suppress a proposal which merely reduces rich pickings.

'A Citizens' Income will frighten foreign investors away.'

This is a possible consequence of the admitted fact that the CI entails high taxation. Having regard to the Tragedy of the Commons, 'inward investment' is a mixed blessing, often capricious in its nature. A sustainable economy would instead aim for local self sufficiency. However, a rapid withdrawal would be problematic, and as I shall argue later, it would be unwise even for a Green society to drive cutting edge technology away. The explanation in the previous chapter that the CI is only a rearrangement of existing taxation would presumably not mollify the decision-makers in question. But I call as witnesses for the defence my accusers in an earlier case. If critics are right, most wages will go down. This may or may not reassure overseas investors, but it will certainly be beneficial for labour intensive environmentally friendly businesses. In so far as foreign investment might be withdrawn (too quickly?), that would certainly be aggravated by the existence of a minimum wage.

High taxation might however induce very high earners to emigrate to shores where a neo-liberal ideology still prevailed. If there is a danger of this being too widespread, it will be at its worst at the outset, when the difficulty of 'selling' the Citizens' Income principle is at its greatest. In the long term, once established the CI could form the basis for a consensus where this was less likely, and eventually less feasible.

'The Citizens' Income will have a centralizing tendency.'

The size of the unit on which the CI is based can be whatever people want it to be. I have assumed that the present unit, namely Britain in our case, would be the simplest choice, certainly until people have got used to the idea. The larger the unit however, the greater the consistency and sharing of resources. Smaller units might mean that relatively affluent areas kept their wealth to themselves, and it could cause unnecessary migration to already crowded areas. Fraudulent claims near boundaries might also be a problem. It might be possible to deal with these problems by applying the same principle as between localities – block payments from affluent to poorer areas – but this could be quite complex, and would cause constant tension. It could even be that a CI would have to be introduced Europe-wide.[8] If there is a perception, contrary to the arguments in this and the next chapter, that it would put taxation up more than it would 'drive wages down', the Tragedy of the Commons might rear its ugly head and threaten the relocation of international capital.

'How will the Citizens' Income be introduced?'

It could be phased in by age groups. Simply changing the name from 'Jobseeker's Allowance' to 'Citizens' Income', and not prosecuting for working at the same time would be a *de facto* introduction, though the transition would be uncontrolled, and might be quite rapid! I personally favour Jonathan Dixon's suggestion referred to at the end of the last chapter: gradually introduce tax credits which if unused, could be reclaimed as a rebate. Dixon has refined this proposal into four-stages: extend the Working Families Tax Credit to all individuals; reduce the qualifying hours from 16 to 8 per week; define workers to include carers, volunteers and students; and increase the Retirement (Old Age) Pension to the level of the Minimum Income Guarantee proposed by the Labour government in 2001 (approximately £95pw).

Finally, I must reiterate that the cost to better off taxpayers, though larger, and in the opposite direction to the tax-cutting auction which neo-liberalism advocates, is affordable. That would only cease to be so if the 3:1 ratio shown in Table 3 in the last chapter shrank significantly. Provided we look after our assets and the biosphere properly, that need never happen.

Notes and References

1   Working Families Tax Credit is withdrawn at the rate of 55%, so even with a flat rate tax of 43% the family in the example would be likely to gain still further. This example pre-dates minor changes in the 2002 Budget, but as pointed out elsewhere, changes in the details (e.g. Minimum Wage rate) will not affect the principle outlined.

2   De Jager, Nicole et al (1995), *Negative Income Tax in a mini Welfare State: a simulation with MIMIC* (1997) Research Memorandum no.112, Centraal Planbureau, Sdu Publishers, Den Haag. A computer simulation of a partial Basic Income.

3   Arguably progressive tax rates subsidise employers to some extent.

4   Douthwaite, Richard (1999), *The Ecology of Money*, Green Books, Dartington, p24.

5   This need not affect payment direct to landlords on behalf of vulnerable tenants.

6   The main beneficiaries of the CAP are large, rather than family-size farms.

7   For a philosophical justification of a Citizens' Income independently of ecological issues, read van Parijs, Philippe (1995), *Real Freedom for All*, Oxford University Press.

8   Alison Marshall has suggested in correspondence that the unit for the CI should include all areas that share the same currency, on the grounds that exchange rates, interest rates, etc. cannot be used to manage differences in local economies, so wealth should be redistributed within the currency area to reduce the differences instead.

VIII

The wider implications

How the Citizens' Income can form the basis for a paradigm shift

(i) Reconciling old adversaries

A few years ago a young German Green was invited to a UK Green Party Conference. All went well until he happened to mention in passing that his party was in favour of NATO. There was shocked silence. He was not from the better known Bundnis 90 Die Grünen (B90DG), but the Ökologische Demokratische Partei (ÖDP). In Germany there are two Green Parties, a large, well known one which is clearly 'left wing' and a smaller one which is predominantly to be found in the south of Germany where the conservative CDU/CSU parties are strongest. To begin with there was only one party, Die Grünen, but even though all claimed global environmental concerns as their purpose, the differences were too great. Die Grünen advocated gay and lesbian rights, for example, whereas the ÖDP stressed traditional family values. On the issue of NATO, the issue is less clear, especially since B90DG (the name since German reunification) were ambiguous as the possibility of joining the government became closer. But there is no way the UK Green Party could countenance support for the North Atlantic Treaty Organization. That these differences between 'left' Greens and 'right' Greens are taken seriously enough to prevent mutual co-operation on the central issue of sustainability worries me more than do the bones of contention.

This seems to be a widespread syndrome. In France, the General election in 1993 was contested by two parties, Les Verts and Mouvement des Ecologistes Independants (MEI). MEI was smaller, and unhappy with the strategy of an alliance with the left. Consequently both failed to make any impact. It is claimed that this split has since been healed, and Dominique Voynet, the Green presidential candidate in 1995, subsequently became a member of the Government. She identifies herself as left of centre. Again, more left Greens than right, as predicted in Chapter 5. I understand that a similar pattern has occurred in Austria, where once again there is only one effective, leftish party.[1] In the Netherlands there is a party with parliamentary representation which actually calls itself 'Green-Left', and an ineffectual 'Green Party' which presumably includes people who cannot bear to be so labelled. The same problem has even emerged in the United States. According to reports in the British press, Ralph Nader, the Green candidate in the 2000 Presidential election, made little mention of climate change, stressing instead that he was for the little guy against the giant corporations. Fine, but not surprisingly, he is generally assumed to have taken votes exclusively from the Democrat, Al Gore. Gore had a relatively good environmental record, and was arguably deprived in a knife-edge result of what would otherwise have been a clear-cut victory over George W. Bush, who most emphatically did not.

Retaining conventional allegiances is understandable where favourable voting systems allow the luxury of gaining representation without too radical a re-think. However, even under the unforgiving electoral system in Britain there has been an attempt to set up a 'Conserver' party, expressly appealing to Conservatives. The possible grain of truth in its claim that the Green Party had been sidetracked from the main business of saving the planet would not justify splitting the movement. Again, its support was miniscule even when compared with the none too numerous Green Party.

It should follow from the story so far that a basis for rapprochement between Greens from different backgrounds can be found in what I have called the Siane strategy, of which the Citizens' Income is the immediate practical embodiment. A paradigm shift is something which takes place inside a person's head which becomes powerful when it happens inside millions of heads. The first step is for people who already regard themselves as Green to think this through. They have to undergo a mini paradigm shift in no longer feeling instinctive hostility to or suspicion of people who come to the Green door with baggage of which they disapprove, more often than not 'right wing' baggage. They can and must do this because the newcomers have a bigger and more difficult paradigm shift to work through, but not so difficult as the total acceptance of socialism which some Greens insist on. Instead of repelling them, Greens have the task of helping newcomers through *their* paradigm shift.

This line of argument is not entirely theoretical. At the General Election in May 1979, the Ecology Party (i.e. the Green Party) fielded 52 candidates. At that stage, the only public perception of the Party was that it wanted to save the environment. In 8 seats won by Labour, the average

Ecology poll was 376, or 0.99%. In the 44 seats taken by the Conservatives, the average Ecology vote was 828: 1.57%. Compare this with the result in May 1997, when perceptions could be based on the Party's track record. The average Green vote was 1.61 % in Labour held seats, and 1.22% in Conservative territory.[2] I believe that parliamentary elections are more revealing than others because they are the elections to which the public attaches the most importance, and local Green efforts have less effect on the overall result.

I am not here primarily concerned with the reasons for the failure of the Green Party vote to rise higher than 1.38% in 1997, as compared to 1.43% at the 'cold' start in 1979, but with the switch of support. For me it is evidence of the reluctance of both sides to leave behind old allegiances. Understandable, but regrettable. In 1979 the Green Party was completely new, and unknown, except for its concern about the environment and the Planet. That was still largely true at the time of the 1989 European election 'breakthrough', but by 1997 it was recognized as clearly left of (the old) centre. It gained some former Labour voters, but a significant part of that original goodwill in the Tory Shires located it in an uncongenial part of the old political spectrum, and quietly melted away.[3]

There are two other clues, on issues only indirectly related to the question of sharing strategies, which nevertheless correlate to a degree with traditional loyalties and assumptions. They also demonstrate the 'paradigm shift' problems which I am trying to address. In 1982 the Ecology Party adopted unilateral nuclear disarmament as Party policy. When canvassing during the next local elections, I had doors literally slammed in my face, with 'You lot would let the Russians in!' where the previous year I had been given a hearing. For two years I had been pursuing the gradual process of leading those I had identified as likely to respond to the Green message. The doors where simply the physical expression of minds which had been firmly closed to any further movement.

The process whereby the Ecology Party had arrived at that decision was instructive. 1979 saw the first conference after the Party had achieved national awareness in the General Election earlier that year. It was therefore by far the largest conference to date, with a huge proportion of new recruits. In a debate on unilateral nuclear disarmament, opinion split 50-50, and was quite polarized. In 1982, the decision was virtually consensual! I have two possible explanations, one depressing, and the other more optimistic. I believe that both were at work. Between 1979 and 1982 there will have been a degree of the self-selection which I have just postulated: ex-Conservative sympathisers drifting back to their roots, and a tendency for former Labour supporters to be recruited. On the other hand I was one of those who voted for conventional 'wisdom' in 1979. I was motivated to stay and discuss, and I went through precisely the kind of mini paradigm shift I believe can occur wholesale. Unfortunately, I was only too well aware that for the voters back home this was somewhat premature.

This area of tension between existing Greens and potential right of centre recruits is thrown into relief by the recent military conflicts in the Balkans, Afghanistan and Iraq. It has occurred to me that there is an exact parallel with sharing strategies. Although complete sharing is consistent with sustainability whereas unbridled competition is not, the optimum basis for sustainability is a combination which incorporates an element of competition within defined limits. In the same way, pacifism is entirely compatible with an ecological philosophy, whereas aggression clearly is not. However, a common and successful strategy found in the animal kingdom is the 'retaliator' strategy: never be the aggressor, but if attacked, it is legitimate to make the aggressor regret it, and to prevent him from gaining by it. As a sustainable society and ecological principles gain acceptance, the difference in practice between the 'retaliator' strategy and pacifism could be reduced to vanishing point. Green attitudes have to take into account the often dubious motives and actions of the USA, but if the Green movement presents a pacifist image by always opposing war, it will deter moderate ex-Conservatives from moving towards a Green paradigm just as an insistence on Socialism will do the same.

The second 'right of centre' example concerns foxhunting. I have heard Tracy, Marchioness of Worcester speak, and I have spoken to her personally. We share substantially the same Green paradigm. She had been proposed as a candidate on the Green Party list in the South-West Region for the 1999 European Election. However, her background is that of the landed gentry, and she made no secret of her own pro-hunting views. Green Party members in the region were sharply and evenly divided, and she withdrew from the list as a result.[4] Personally, I am against foxhunting. Philosophically, for me needless cruelty to animals is inconsistent with Green principles. I therefore believe – and hope – that there is scope here for the kind of mini paradigm shift among that section of society which has hitherto seen nothing wrong with hunting as sport. But foxhunting is not a core Green issue *politically*. It is not inconsistent with a sustainable society, so such a paradigm shift is not essential. We shall not know to what extent it will take place until we allow people like Tracy Worcester to begin the gradual process of leading the large section of society who respect them towards a Green world view.

As I have hinted, there are other areas in which 'left of centre' Greens will have to make allowances. Most of these can be postponed,[5] but there is one piece of conservative 'baggage' which will not merely be allowed in, it is in my view integral to the Green paradigm from the outset: opposition to the minimum wage. I have outlined the practical aspects of the case against the minimum wage in the last Chapter. I shall now try to illustrate its role as a litmus test for the paradigm shift.

A minimum wage is effective only for those who have a job. Full employment *almost* happened once in Britain, around 1961. Yet a minimum wage at a level which Trade Unions regard as satisfactory could risk making some, perhaps many jobs uneconomical. I have yet to hear how this could be avoided, *except on the back of economic growth* regardless of environmental damage, or of any considerations other than job creation. So a minimum wage is potentially inimical to a sustainable society. A minimum wage is based on two assumptions. The first is the very reasonable proposition that everyone should have enough to live on. The second assumption is that this should be achieved entirely through paid employment. That purpose is better fulfilled by the Citizens' Income. If a living income must be tied to a job, then jobs – at high hourly rates- must be found whatever the consequences.

To those Greens who have difficulty in letting go of the minimum wage as an article of faith, I must ask these questions:

- You want to abolish poverty. How will the minimum wage add to the effect of the Citizens' Income *in a zero growth economy*? Remember, the CI gives the unemployed and part time workers bargaining power they have never had before, so the answer cannot include 'It will prevent exploitation.'

- How do *you* respond to the charge that you are penalizing your old enemies, the employers, rather than finding the best way of rescuing disadvantaged members of society without adding to pressure for inappropriate economic growth?

Just as Green ex-conservatives will have to accept that their gut conviction that everyone should have to stand on their own two feet would cause inexorable pressure to forge ahead with economic growth, so Green ex-socialists must face the same reality in relation to one of their cherished aims.[6]

One reason why the Citizens' Income has had such a hard time in making headway until now is actually related to its hidden strength as the embodiment of the Siane strategy. I claim that it is a fusion – a welding of the hitherto apparently antipathetic concepts of social justice and private enterprise. But those on both sides who do not yet recognize the environment and threats to the biosphere as requiring such a reconciliation will go on fighting the old battles. Those who have taken the trouble to consider the Citizens' Income immediately see its advantages – to the other side. Thus the majority of Conservatives notice only that it would be redistributive, whilst Trade Unionists fear its potential for 'driving wages down'. There is even a member of the Green Party – his calibre is indicated by the fact that he has worked as a researcher in Parliament – who started as a supporter of the Citizens' Income. He turned against it for no better reason than that he discovered it was also supported by some Conservatives!

The early slogan 'Not left, not right, but forward!' was trite, and has been quietly dropped of late. 'Both left *and* right, *and* forward' still doesn't quite 'gel', but something along those lines could encapsulate what is needed. It will take time, but eventually a willingness to talk to, and a wish to seek agreement with moderates among old enemies about traditional differences over a whole range of issues will come. NATO, nuclear (and general) disarmament, foxhunting, the monarchy, law and order issues, private education, the health service and so on all have varying degrees of relevance to the core issue of sustainability. Co-operation with new-found allies will in time cease to feel like sacrificing one's principles. I have already observed such shifts in thinking where new members of the Green Party have not met with too much hostility to their original point of view, and have themselves been sufficiently motivated to talk matters through.

But to reach out to former enemies will still feel like a betrayal of principles to many who quite genuinely think of themselves as Green. At worst, it is a question of priorities. I personally fear that the Green movement cannot make significant progress until this rapprochement does take place. Suppose for example, that John Gummer applied to join the Green Party. During his stint as a Conservative Minister, latterly of the Environment, his personal paradigm visibly shifted greenwards. Would he be made welcome? The Green paradigm – the view that we must tailor our whole way of life to the limitations of the biosphere – can and must achieve a mass following, but I fear that it will take a great deal longer than necessary without the help of allies who for example expect foxhunting to remain a permanent feature of country life. I am quite clear where my priorities lie. As I have tried to point out in Chapter 3, refusal to co-operate across these ancient battle-lines is not merely not an option, it is downright irresponsible. The malign forces which will take advantage of this failure are already mobilizing. The longer we leave it, the easier it will be for extremists to appeal to the destructive side of our nature.

(ii) An alternative to neo-liberalism for ordinary people

The 'Good Life' was a television series first broadcast in 1975. In it a draughtsman with good promotion prospects in a secure but basically meaningless job suddenly went through the paradigm shift, though of course the programme did not use that expression. He and his long-suffering wife went the whole hog, abandoning his potentially high flying career, and turning their beautiful garden into an organic farm, pig slurry and all. It was a clever combination of the yearning to get out of the materialistic rat race, and the limitations of trying to do anything about it as an individual. The series was a great success, and has been repeated endlessly. Needless to say, it has not noticeably brought the rest of the nation any closer to a paradigm shift. An essential element in the humour was that we are all locked into the system willy nilly.

But this is where the Citizens' Income comes in. The beauty of it is the flexibility it makes possible. It doesn't have to be all or nothing. Each individual can begin to re-think her/his situation and make gradual changes, first in their thinking, and then in what they do, and the plans they make. For some it may well be that to live on the CI after earning an above average wage will be worth the relief from stress. For others it will be a few hours less, a less stressful job nearer home, a voluntary post, or one which pays a pittance, but which gives a sense of personal worth. At this stage we are still a long way from challenging the Tragedy of the Commons, but imperceptibly, millions of people will take advantage of this new opportunity to *think* differently. Above all, security is no longer bound up with the rat race, and the chase for material possessions. As individuals, people can begin to prefer values other than consumer durables. Consumerism will become optional, instead of compulsory, as it is to all intents and purposes at present. In short, people will find themselves able to contemplate, perhaps not an out and out 'Space Capsule Earth' paradigm at this stage, but certainly a sustainable, less fraught one.

All this is the consequence of adopting the Siane strategy – security guaranteed, anything else is up to you. We do not want to suppress consumerism completely. The Siane strategy does require something above basic needs to aim for. Moreover, as I shall discuss later, conventional concerns about too low a level of demand cannot be dismissed entirely. But the difference between the Siane strategy and the arrangement we have at present cannot be stressed too strongly. Instead of flexibility, you are either included or excluded from society. If you have the misfortune to get yourself excluded, society says to you 'Which would you like this week, some money or your self-respect? If you take the money, we shall call it a hand out, despise you, and penalize you if you do anything to help yourself.' Fear of this fate ensures that it takes a very brave or eccentric person to even think of opting out of consumerism.

Another factor which will contribute to this trend is a reduction in crime. Cultural factors will ensure that it takes a long time before house burglaries, thefts from cars and the like subside, but drawing on my experience as a Probation Officer I predict that they will. In the mid 1980s, Mrs Thatcher, in one of her determined pushes towards the 'right wing' no-sharing pole, withdrew benefits *entirely* from school-leavers up to 18. The theory was that it would make them determined to find work. Indeed some were, but the real world soon blunted that. It came as no surprise to some of us working in the field that car crime and housebreaking by this age group rose dramatically over the next three or four years. Once a pattern like this has developed, it tends to perpetuate itself, but at least the Citizens' Income removes the poverty and demoralisation which was the mainspring driving the rise in property crime caused by that tightening of the screw. The payoff for householders and car owners is that as the CI does begin to influence values and attitudes, insurance rates will fall.

The next phase will be due to another consequence of the Citizens' Income's tendency to take the pressure off demand. We have seen that it will enhance ecologically sound activity, such as house insulation, repair work, recycling and so on, but overall it will have two effects which will tend to cancel each other out. If as expected by Trade Union critics of a CI, hourly wage rates go down on average, this will allow prices and costs to manufacturers and service providers to fall. Consumer spending *would* slacken slightly as income falls in response to the more relaxed atmosphere which the CI makes possible, but more attractive prices will work in the opposite direction. So there will be neither a boom nor a recession. There will still be much the same amount of cash flowing through the economy, though a *slightly* lower proportion of it will go on luxuries.

All these effects will be negligible to the point of imperceptibility, certainly in the early stages in the domestic British market where it is just a matter of 'roundabouts and swings' anyway. But consider the effect on external trade. Exports will become, again *slightly* more competitive abroad due to the lower wage costs, but the imperceptibly reduced purchasing power will inhibit imports, as will any trend towards less consumerism, though this may amount to much the same thing. The potential effect is that of knocking 2p off the price of a packet of soap as compared to all its rivals. If Britain becomes slightly less consumerist internally, but retains, indeed marginally improves its capacity to supply the rest of the world with unabated demands, it will suddenly find itself in a strong trading position! This is of course not what Green politics is supposed to be about, but as we saw in considering the Tragedy of the Commons, if you wish to be in a position to influence events when a foreseeable crisis is looming, economic strength may be no bad thing.

Unfortunately for Britain plc, the advantage will be short-lived. If the Citizens' Income does have this effect, other trading nations will not take long to follow suit. Of course the CI will not be introduced with equal ease universally. The internal situations in the 'Asian Tiger' economies, Japan, Western Europe and the USA are all different. Countries such as Sweden and Germany have traditionally had generous social security systems. Until now this has inhibited their willingness to consider a Citizens' Income, because the cost to those in higher income brackets would be higher than in Britain, if the rate is to match their higher unemployment benefit levels. However, these economies, and hence their social security systems have come under strain recently. Faced with a range of unpalatable alternatives to stave off a crisis, a Citizens' Income might not seem as politically impossible as it did, particularly if Britain had shown what its effects were likely to be in practice.

Of course the big challenges are the USA and Japan. Japan has shown herself adept at responding very quickly to innovations by others. The Japanese too are finding that it may not be possible to rely on providing everyone with a job within some family firm or giant corporation. Supreme pragmatists that they are, I believe that the Japanese will seamlessly adopt the Citizens' Income. They may not even need a British precedent. The USA will of course have strong ideological objections to a CI. Nevertheless I would not expect them to dally too long if they see the rest of the world stealing a march. This potential development is crucial as a catalyst for the establishment of a sustainable society. Not until the general population of the USA and Japan have been offered a basis on which to consider any alternative to the competitive consumerist rat race is there much prospect of a world wide consensus on sustainability.

I am well aware that this prediction is quite audacious. However, my confidence is based on the soundness of the 'Siane' strategy. So important is the quotation in Chapter 4, that I must repeat it (and my italics) here:

In many societies there is a sharp distinction between the way food and other goods are exchanged. ... Among the Siane of New Guinea ... the notion underlying the basis of distribution of food is that of equal shares. ...[whereas]... Luxury goods are exchanged according to self-interest in a nearly free market situation ...

An important by-product of such systems concerns the homogeneity of societies. The more equitable the system for the distribution of food and other necessities, *the greater the identity of interest within the society when faced with ecological problems.*

In other words, this strategy allows a slackening of individual material expectations without insecurity, and that is what can, not will, make it slightly easier to export and harder to import. In passing, I must yet again confront the minimum wage. This predicted effect of the Citizens' Income – giving one country a temporary trading advantage – is by no means inevitable. It will be barely perceptible at first, and a minimum wage must seriously hamper any such possibility.

A more formidable issue which must be confronted is the current consensus that takes economic growth for granted. I shall return in the final chapter to a discussion of the circumstances in which growth might be feasible and acceptable. In the absence of the Siane strategy in some shape or form, periodic glitches when growth fails to materialize have always caused hardship. The Siane strategy means that growth can no longer be defended as the only way to generate wealth and alleviate poverty, something it has not generally achieved in any case. But on the other hand, the Citizens' Income ensures that a basic level of economic activity will always take place. The instability which inevitably dogs a system which depends on growth need never occur again.

I must make it clear that I am *not* advocating the 'deep ecology' position of emulating primitive societies, except in this single respect of adopting their sharing strategy. I maintain only that the Siane strategy can be extrapolated and applied to modern complex societies. However, the whole process depends on feedback. The Citizens' Income will *allow*, not cause, a slackening of individuals' demands on the environment (though they can still produce goods for others). It will also allow, not cause, people currently in or just above the Poverty Trap to begin to be troubled more about wider ecological considerations than their own immediate insecurities. It will do this by asking those higher up the income scale to accept what for most of them will be a marginal percentage reduction in income.

It depends on the paradigm shift. For anyone who still subscribes to the neo-liberal paradigm, or just has a conventional unthinking reliance on economic growth, the CI will fail to have any of these predicted effects. Indeed, for the more affluent, even a 1% drop in income will immediately alienate them from the whole idea. But the minority among the affluent who already have a 'sustainability' paradigm in their heads will accept their marginal losses cheerfully. They will do so because they recognize that they are getting value for money in the shape of recruits from among the low paid who can now afford to join them in worrying about the environment. But above all, taken in conjunction with the principle of localization,[7] the CI offers a blueprint to which those uneasy about the current dominance of trade over all else, but who are still unconvinced that the need for sustainability is urgent, can relate. It does not need to happen in practice first for large numbers of the conventional majority to visualize, and then come over to an ecological paradigm. Once the Citizens' Income, or at least some version of the Siane strategy is common as a concept world-wide, the scene is set for a paradigm shift to a consensus which takes care of the only biosphere we possess.

Notes and References

1   From information supplied by Hazel Dawe, Canterbury Green Party.
2   The difference becomes more marked if the marginals, i.e seats where the result was perceived to be in doubt, are removed. In 1979 in five 'safe' Labour' strongholds, defined as with majorities greater than 5,000, the average Ecology poll was 405, or exactly 1.00%. In 39 safe Conservative seats, with the same definition, (but bearing in mind that the tide was running in their favour), the Ecology average was 865, or 1.64%. In 1997 in 27 Labour seats (all but two with majorities in excess of 11,000) the Green vote was 801, or 1.88%. In 20 safe Conservative seats (with the same definition) it was 676 (1.22%).
3   See Appendix I for evidence from the 2001 general election. The pendulum appears to have begun to swing back.
4   I personally believe that this deprived the Green Party of a third MEP. In the election, the No. 1 Green candidate, David Taylor, comparatively unknown and certainly without Tracy Worcester's influence, polled 8%, the Green Party's highest percentage nationally.
5   I touch on these in Chapter 11.
6   For a 'right wing' perspective on the CI and the arguments against a minimum wage in this context, see Brittan, Samuel (1995), *Capitalism with a Human Face*, Edward Elgar Publishing, Cheltenham.
7   Hines, Colin (2000), *Localization – a Global Manifesto*, Earthscan, London.

IX

Tactical and strategic implications

Getting to grips with the Tragedy

Conventional parties are prevented from being serious about Green principles and policies because the Green paradigm accepts certain constraints which they ignore. At first sight, this does not seem to be a problem. MORI and ICM polls indicate majority support for a whole raft of Green policies:[1] renationalizing the railways (76%); scrapping the national roads programme and investing the money in public transport (61%); protection for small producers against transnationals (87%); and unease as to globalization (80%), among several others less directly related to sustainability. Opposition to genetically modified crops could almost certainly have been added to this list. But for those who have not gone through the paradigm shift to a Green world view, on balance the package will be unpopular because conventional parties must always be able to outbid a Green party in terms of consumer-oriented promises. For example they will say that petrol prices *can* be kept down, and they will ignore any conflict between measures necessary to halt global warming and economic expansion. In the longer term, the basic Green premise that population cannot go on expanding indefinitely will not be popular among those not yet through the paradigm shift.

The Tragedy of the Commons (the rule that the first to observe ecological limitations put themselves at a disadvantage, whilst those who are successful in achieving growth the longest will be in the strongest economic position when the problems come home to roost), aggravates this difficulty into a world-wide problem of extremely worrying proportions. The Tragedy is expressed in the mantra 'International competitiveness'. Loss of market share looms larger than loss of biodiversity. Globalization amounts to a giant, but still unacknowledged game of poker. If the major players recognize it as such, they certainly do not admit it.

A couple of issues which are or have recently been topical as I write serve as typical examples. The government introduced a levy on office and some industrial heating, to encourage insulation etc, and discourage greenhouse gases. The intensive horticulture industry was angry. Surely this had been applied to them by mistake? The hard fact is that methods currently used in intensive horticulture are unsustainable, but are comparable rules being simultaneously imposed in the Netherlands and elsewhere?

In September 2000 a rise in fuel prices caused by demand outstripping the oil supply sparked an extreme reaction by fishermen, HGV drivers, farmers and taxi drivers in France. Their blockades were supported by the populace at large. Even the relatively low key 'Dump the Pump' campaign in Britain protesting about high vehicle fuel prices relative to those on the near continent was supported by Don Foster, the Liberal Democrat spokesperson on the environment. This conflicts with any claims he may have made on the need for traffic reduction. Tactically he was of course wise. Much more virulent fuel blockades spread across Europe shortly afterwards. As long as there is an element of potential unpopularity in any given measure of ecological restraint, particularly when it threatens 'business as usual', politicians will dodge the issue, and the pressure of the Tragedy will continue to be inexorable.

The Citizens' Income is a prime example of this problem of initial unpopularity. The realization that social equity is a pre-requisite for sustainability is slowly gaining ground. Hitherto, it has been widely assumed that this must mean Socialism. However, the environmentally unreconstructed majority will continue to assess any proposal strictly on the basis 'Am I financially better or worse off?' Both Socialism and the Citizens' Income fail this test for any affluent individual unsympathetic to Green aims. The CI is potentially more popular than Socialism, but it will benefit a minority considerably, to the slight detriment of the majority. The Liberal Democrats got cold feet about the CI for this reason, and even the Green Party has invariably flinched from featuring it prominently at election times.

Green Parties have to live in the world as it is. The German Greens would like to put greater pressure on their SPD coalition partners, but they cannot ask for decisions which would put Germany at an economic disadvantage, just because in an ideal world that disadvantage should only be short term. Most of the German public was already irritated by their demands for 'Ökosteuer' (eco-taxation, primarily on petrol) and at best apathetic about 'Atomausstieg' (closing nuclear power stations) during the campaign prior to the national election in September 1998. As a result of these policies featuring and being attacked during the campaign, despite extensive media coverage their support actually fell from 7.3% (7.9% in the west, 4.3% in the east) in 1994 to 6.7% (7.3% in the west, 4.1% in the east) in 1998. This disturbing reality was masked by the euphoria of forming a coalition with the SPD, and entering government for the first time.

The shift to a 'Space Capsule Earth', or at least a 'sustainability' paradigm will not happen overnight. Only individuals who have gone through this paradigm shift can be expected to see the sense in and accept effective ecological solutions. But to be rational, and to protect short term interests, most of the important solutions will have to wait until 'mutual coercion mutually agreed upon' is a realistic possibility. It is far too much to ask any party founded on any principle other than sustainability to even think of offering sustainable solutions to a public which still takes the status quo for granted.

Such a course will not be easy for a Green party. At present the dominant approach within the Green Party in England is to start from grass roots and gain representation at local level. This is 'right' in the sense that it is the most realistic level to target, borne out by the slowly increasing degree of success. But it is laborious (nothing wrong with that if it gets results), patchy, and limited to issues decided at local level. Publicity is restricted to areas where Greens are active. Above all, due to the tactical conflict between problems perceived by the public now and fundamental aims, this approach does nothing to deal with global problems, and the public is not offered a world view to consider as an alternative to business as usual.

I have just quoted the experience of Bundnis 90 die Grünen in Germany, where pressing for petrol taxes arguably caused a fall in their support. What I wonder is the experience of British Greens on 'hung' councils (holding the balance of power)? How will they, or have they, handled planning issues such as a large potential employer offering to locate in their district, on condition that a substantial chunk of Green Belt is made available? (Or threatening to re-locate *out* if it is not?) Dare they risk the wrath of a public which still does not understand what Green politics is *really* about? Although the roads programme may be unpopular in the abstract, the widespread *local* condemnation of the decision in July 2001 *not* to build a Hastings by-pass gives a flavour of what to expect.

A strategy pursued by some in the wider Green movement has been to work unobtrusively within the corridors of power, or to try to influence parties holding or likely to hold power. This has been the policy of Friends

of the Earth, a quite successful campaigning and awareness raising organization for many years. There are instances where they could claim to
have exerted pressure successfully. But others have charted much better
than I could the lack of progress towards sustainability under either
Conservative or Labour governments. As already explained the 'Tragedy'
dogs this approach. There is of course a Green Group in the European
Parliament, which since June 1999 includes two UK Green MEPs, Jean
Lambert and Caroline Lucas. At present, they have a very full agenda
dealing with things which are achievable, for example a proposed airport
landing tax. They can begin the process of setting up an infrastructure
which will make sustainability possible and which removes obstacles to it,
but sooner or later they too must face the dilemmas posed by the Tragedy.

I first went out 'doorstepping' for what is now called the Green Party
in the General Election in February 1974, full of fresh enthusiasm, and
only recently though the paradigm shift myself. I discovered fairly quickly
that less than 1% of the general population (at least in that particular
suburban area of Leeds) already held some sort of Green paradigm.[2]
However, up to 10% were sympathetic to some degree. They listened to
my arguments, and could I believed be ripe for the paradigm shift, given
enough media exposure to our case.

What the observant reader will have noticed is that 90% had no interest
in Green issues. In fact at least 10% were *opposed* to what I was saying. It
may have been that particular area, a predominantly Jewish suburb with
a high proportion of self-made entrepreneurs who had arrived as refugees
from Europe and pulled themselves up by their bootstraps, but I met
'Bernard' from Chapter 2 several times. It was self-evident to them that
humankind would always have the ingenuity to outwit the eco-crisis I was
needlessly worried about.

There is wider awareness of Green issues now, but the situation has not
improved dramatically. In the February 1974 general election, PEOPLE
(i.e. Green Party) candidates in comparable contests (i.e where there was
a Liberal candidate) achieved approximately 0.8% on average. In 1979,
this rose to 1.43%. In Appendix I, I offer evidence that our basic support
at the 2001 general election where local factors and activity were either
absent, or overpowered by the 'squeeze' in marginal constituencies, then
stood at 1.54%. Typically we achieve around 3.5% with 'paper candidates'
in council elections where there are no special factors.[3] Polls taken at the
time of the oil refinery blockades in September 2000 revealed 88% public
support for them in France, and between 78% and 84% support in Britain.
This indicates to me that the 10% level of potential sympathy in 1974 for

what we would now call the Green message, which must have seemed quite outlandish at the time, cannot even now be higher than 16%, or 22% at best. The paradigm shift is happening, but very slowly.

For me, it is axiomatic that only a Green Party can be the vehicle for effective policies aimed at creating a sustainable society. Sooner or later there will have to be governments with a coherent set of policies based on sustainability as their central principles. Only on this basis can the Tragedy of the Commons be realistically challenged. But it took me a long time to realize that not everyone in the Green movement shares my belief that the Tragedy of the Commons will seriously hamper real progress until the paradigm shift has taken place extensively. What seemed to me the obvious strategy back in those early 1974 'doorstepping' days was to target the 10% who even then, long before the environment became topical, were almost ready to be led through the paradigm shift, at any rate up to the point where a significant proportion of them could be relied on to vote Green consistently, even in parliamentary elections. This is not fanciful. During the 1940s 50s and 60s the Liberal Party had a loyal following who would vote for them in all elections without the slightest expectation of any tangible result.

What I believe the Green Party should have been doing as a priority throughout, is to use the media, and any other means at their disposal to bring the Green paradigm to the notice of potential sympathizers, and then to help them through the paradigm shift. The Citizens' Income, in tandem with localization, purely as ideas, can make this strategy a practical proposition. It will allow individuals to reconsider their personal goals, and in due course recognize and then welcome political changes which for many would feel threatening without a sense of basic security, or at least not in their interests. I believe the Citizens' Income can do this because it is the embodiment of a strategy which has been tried and tested by societies which have already successfully negotiated the transition back from expansion to sustainability.

A consistent 5-8% support in parliamentary elections would not merely save deposits, it would be sufficient to give the Green Party regular media exposure. We would of course always remind people that our central purpose was sustainability, and outline policies on economics, transport, energy and housing which make sense on this basis. But if this media opportunity were to be used primarily to explain the effect of the Citizens' Income on individuals, the 16% or more who are ready to consider the paradigm shift could be persuaded to take the plunge, and the numbers on the threshold steadily increased. I have already identified two obvious target groups. On the one hand, there are those who will be able, for the first time, to raise their heads above their day to day financial preoccupations, many of whom probably do not even figure in the 16%. On the other hand there are those who are worried about climate change, but who would object to losing out under a Citizens' Income if this connection had not been established. I believe that real power can only be achieved by a Green Party when the public has had a chance to consider this initially unpopular combination of ideas discussed in depth over a period of time.

Both Labour and Conservative parties have from time to time toyed with Green ideas. To begin with, each had core principles – social justice and private enterprise respectively, though both have become somewhat vague about them recently. Both occasionally feel the need to paint themselves Green, but in addition to 'Tragedy'-related problems there were bound to be difficulties in reconciling this with core principles. If it were possible to usher in Green policies *without* a paradigm shift inside millions of heads, the Liberal Party would have taken on the Green mantle in the 1970s, because they and their successors are primarily opportunists. The Green Party has one thing in common with Labour and Conservatives (as they were) which the Lib Dems do not share – we too have a core principle – sustainability – which can be a drawback.[4] It means that you cannot always be pragmatic, if an issue (e.g. petrol prices or air travel) crops up on which your basic principles have something to say.

Of course the Liberal Democrats do indeed claim to be the 'Green' Party. In 1973-74, I rushed round appealing to anyone who would listen to join our new ecology based party. All rejected the proposition as unnecessary, and far too huge an undertaking. At that time the only 'Green' Party anywhere in the world was the Values party in New Zealand. No one seemed to think of the *Conservatives* as an appropriate vehicle, though they even had advocates of the Citizens' Income at the time. A few said I should join the Labour Party, but most of those who professed to be concerned about the possibility of an ecological crisis were members of the Liberal Party. I argued that any party courting immediate popularity in advance of the paradigm shift would be forced to drop Green ideas whenever – inevitably – the drawbacks as seen from a conventional standpoint emerged. Needless to say, I claim that the Liberal/ Social Democrat/ Liberal Democrat record consistently bears out my fears, as do the records of the two larger parties.

The Lib Dem handling of the Citizens' Income is instructive. They adopted the CI as policy in 1990, and featured it in their 1992 Election Manifesto.[5] However, not only did they never see the connection between it and core Green issues, but their strategists realized that on balance it would alienate more voters than it would attract. Their annual conference duly ditched the CI in 1994. For the Green Party, at the outset needing only sufficient support to gain publicity, controversy could actually help to draw attention to our world view, hence my exasperation at the party's repeated timidity in not highlighting the CI.

There are Green policies which any government could implement, and indeed a start has been made. The Home Energy Conservation Act 1997, a Green Party initiative (though you would not know it from our failure to receive public acknowledgement), means that local authorities the length and breadth of Britain are required to help low income households to insulate their homes and save fuel – and carbon dioxide. A massive switch to solar, wind and wave power has enormous potential, and the obstacles are relatively minor. The Airport Landing Tax proposed by the Green Group in the European Parliament is another example. None of these innovations would require a paradigm shift, or a new political party.

At first sight the UK government's participation in the Kyoto Climate Change accords is another, quite far-reaching example. Unfortunately it is not a good one. In so far as they were on course to meet lower greenhouse gas emissions targets, it was done by the 'dash for gas' – converting power stations from coal to North Sea gas. This is the opposite of the way a Green government would have used North Sea gas. Also their apparently brave efforts to reduce, or at least slow down the increase in road traffic were suffering from an attack of cold feet even before the fuel blockades in 2000. Such disappointments are hardly surprising. They will continue until the shift to an ecological paradigm has taken place inside enough heads. I understand why my more practical colleagues are striving to get *something* done at whatever governmental level they can reach. But we remain essentially in the same position as the tribes of Gaul and Britain resisting the Roman Empire: a 'victory' here or there consists of delaying the march of superior forces, not reversing the destruction of the environment, or laying the foundations of a sustainable society.

Alongside the strategy of using our initially limited support to gain publicity, we shall have to be explicit about the Tragedy of the Commons and its ramifications. This will be quite tricky. It entails a promise to voters, whether Green or not, especially to those who are not, that we would never put them at a disadvantage, even in the short term. In other words, whilst we are determined to shout the Green odds from the rooftops, only where there is an immediate advantage in doing so, or at worst only a marginal, short term disadvantage, will we *behave* ecologically. Where necessary, like any rational shepherd in Chapter 2, we may have to act in flat contradiction to our stated aims until we persuade the rest of the world to change its ways with us. In Chapter 2 I gave examples, such as the environmentally unsound, but commercially successful, entertainment and trading complex on the outskirts of the town where I live, and the threat by a bedding manufacturer to re-locate if not given a green field site. The local Green Party would have done itself a great disservice if it had successfully opposed either, and driven profitable, employment providing enterprises elsewhere.

Unfortunately exactly the same principle applies up to and including the international level. Until there is an international Green consensus,[6] it is a fact of life that air transport *will* expand. Whilst Greens must condemn this as lunacy, must we in the meantime insist that the entire profits go to the last to see sense? I have already described this process as akin to a game of poker. Up to a certain point, those who are most successful at expansion, or in capturing 'inward investment' reap rich rewards. It is a game of chance, and already there have been spectacular corporate losers, but there is undoubted skill in judging the point at which this approach becomes folly.

The Green Party has had media opportunities which could have been used to set out this strategy of using minority support to familiarize the public with the Citizens' Income, and its relationship with the more obvious Green issues. We have had several able representatives on BBC *Question Time*. Time after time I have railed at the TV screen, as questions which provided the natural introduction to the approach suggested here were squandered. At the European Election in June 1989 we were presented with a golden opportunity. The environment temporarily became mainstream, and the 10% who sympathized did indeed nearly all vote for us.[7]

For me the experience of the German Greens is depressing evidence in support of my thesis. For personal reasons I receive satellite transmissions of German television programmes, from which it is clear that Bündnis 90 Die Grünen has for years enjoyed consistent media coverage beyond my wildest dreams. Yet as pointed out earlier, far from having extended their potential support, in 1998 their support fell. The recovery in 2002 to 8.6% (9.5% in the West, 4.8% in the East) *might* indicate that perhaps a significant number are indeed approaching the paradigm shift, appalling floods a few weeks before the election having concentrated people's minds. However, most professional pundits considered that personalities having acquitted themselves well in government was a more important factor.

There has of course always been a furious debate among German Greens as to whether to reach for the tantalizingly close levers of power (the 'Realos'), or to stay true to principles (the 'Fundis'). But Germany is a country with a traditionally generous work based social security system, and so it is not the first country where one would expect a Citizens' Income to take root. On the other hand it is countries like Germany and Sweden where people used to feel secure, but are now getting jittery about job security. At all events for understandable tactical reasons Bundnis 90 Die Grünen is not following a strategy of using the CI to coax hearts and minds through the paradigm shift.

Even if a Green Party somewhere achieves an absolute majority, it will still have to face up to the dilemmas posed in Chapter 2. The only way to cope with this that I can see is (a) to persuade more people to think as we do, and (b) to reassure them that they will not be worse off in the short term, even though this may sometimes mean apparently betraying what we stand for.

The most far-reaching effect of the Siane attitude of mind is that it makes possible a slackening of overall demand, and above all, the recognition of the global game of poker for what it is. It will not be easy. The need just noted to safeguard short term economic interests by acting completely contrary to Green aims whilst persuading others will apply internationally with even greater force than it does internally, and I shall expand on this aspect in the next chapters. But there is a real prospect that environmental summits will, unlike Johannesburg in 2002, agree to realistic plans for mutual – enforceable – coercion. At last, in conjunction with localization developing countries will have a frame of reference other than the obscene invitation (duress?) to sit down at the global poker game, and try to take money from the fat guys with marked cards. It is still in the distance, but we are finally in sight of an answer to the Tragedy of the Commons.

Notes and References

1   MORI and ICM polls between January 2000 and June 2001, quoted in *Green World* (The Green Party newsletter), Autumn 2001.
2   In the Leeds North-East Constituency in the February 1974 General Election PEOPLE (now the Green Party) polled 300 votes, or 0.7%.
3   The average poll in 23 wards in West Yorkshire in the May 2000 council elections where no targetting took place was 3.6%.

4   The philosophic introduction to the Liberal Democrat Constitution identifies Liberty as their core principle, but that is less likely to interfere with pragmatism (or opportunism) than are socialism, private enterprise, or sustainability.
5   It was the Liberal Democrats who coined the name Citizens' Income instead of Basic Income.
6   Or a crisis. I discuss that eventuality in Chapter 3.
7   The Green Party's average poll in the June 1989 European Election was 15%. However, as the percentage poll was only a little over half the average poll at a General Election, it was equivalent to 8% in parliamentary terms.

Part Three

Getting from here to there

X

There are no panaceas

A more detailed look at some transitional aspects

(i) Other essentials

The Siane strategy will not cure AIDS. It offers no immediate help in the Middle East, or Northern Ireland, or any of the numerous similar conflicts elsewhere.[1] Nor can it defeat the Tragedy of the Commons unaided. What I believe it can do is open up a range of new options which will bring that stupendous task within the realms of the possible. I claim that the Citizens' Income, or some expression of the Siane strategy is a *sine qua non*, but not that it is the only one. I do not however wish to distract attention from the main purpose of this book by going into great detail on others.

I have already suggested that this book should be read in conjunction with Colin Hines' book on localization.[2] The relationship is that of a hull and superstructure: the Siane strategy is the basic prerequisite. Localization is a detailed policy proposal which might 'float' unaided, but the two will I suggest make a much stronger combination to catch the (world) public imagination than either would alone. Hines offers a detailed picture which gives the lie to the claim that globalization is inevitable. That is accepted by many who should know better, but who think they have no alternative.

The problem remains that like the central proposal in this book, localization may not on its own offer a compelling motive for those in control to take any notice, let alone to relax their grip. Hines seems to rely to some extent on the fact (true) that globalization is already showing signs of coming apart at the seams. This rings familiar alarm bells for me. It was exactly the rationale of the great and the good who tried to recruit me into the Liberal party in 1973. 'Just wait till the *Limits to Growth* predictions come home to roost. Then they will have to put our far-sighted policies into practice.' Unfortunately it doesn't usually happen like that. If people are frightened or impoverished before they have internalized a coherent option, atavistic reflexes will take over. Social breakdown in response to racist demagoguery is far more likely. The less desirable features of localization (a danger recognized by Hines) would be the more apparent.

Another *sine qua non* is population limitation. Population size tends to be overlooked as a component in the Green paradigm because maldistribution is undoubtedly a much more pressing problem at present, aggravated by extravagance and inefficiency. It cannot be stressed too strongly that the stupendous rise in population ever since the invention of agriculture *must* be halted. The last 10,000 years, let alone that last 200, have been exceptional in the context of any history of the world which does not concentrate on humans.[3] This is a major area where Green politics cannot avoid looking negative to anyone who is still on the other side of the paradigm shift. The relationship between expansion and maldistribution was discussed in Chapters 2 to 5. Only pre-agricultural societies have been generally free from hunger except in the higher echelons of more complex societies, and until very recently, only 'primitive' societies have had stable populations. A number of European countries do currently have near equilibrium populations, but far from being seen as a desperately needed achievement, governments are more likely to regard it as a failure to be corrected as soon as possible. And of course they are right. What is the obvious consequence of one country stabilizing its population, if others continue to expand? This should sound familiar. It is a Tragedy.

Population is an area discussion of which is often unwelcome to Greens who start from a 'Social Justice' perspective. This is another topic where a Citizens' Income (or some form of the Siane strategy) renders reasonable 'right wing' ideas which are rightly opposed in its absence. What I would like to see eventually, but would not expect to command a consensus among Greens at present, is a generous CI for a first child, an adequate CI for a second child, but decreasing amounts for subsequent children. The 'break even' point would be at three children. This raises invidious questions. Having argued that a guarantee of security is a necessary precondition for sustainability, including a stable population, here I am introducing a potential cause of *in*security. What about the fourth (or tenth) child in a poor family? But such a modification need not be introduced at the outset. It is the establishment of the Citizens' Income as a principle in people's minds that is urgent. However, by stating the *intention* to introduce such a taper at some point in the future, society could send out a very necessary signal that population increase is an issue. This measure would preserve personal choice and avoid compulsion. If it is effective, further measures may be unnecessary.[4]

Sustainability can never be more than a temporary phenomenon if no heed is paid to numbers. If sheer numbers are not a pressing problem, when will be the right time to stabilize them, to turn away from ever more desperate and risky technical fixes, such as GM crops? Provided we put down markers now, and accept that family size *is* a proper concern for the wider community, problems can be forestalled with relatively mild fiscal measures. No society which has been forced to adopt agriculture (as we saw in Chapter 1 it was never a voluntary choice) has ever found a way to recover its ecological equilibrium. Yet the Siane strategy has always been available. It is only if we ignore population for too long that any of the typical fears of those who resist discussion of this topic need become an issue. House price fluctuations perhaps indicate that population pressure could already be among other, more obvious factors in the more densely populated parts of England. Racist solutions of the worst kind have been part of the armoury of our ancestors for a very long time. It is precisely because I fear this trait in human nature that I wish to ensure that those most prone to it are never given an excuse.

A third *sine qua non* is democracy. Yet again, that this is dealt with in a single paragraph should not be taken to indicate that it is not important. A comprehensive case for democracy as essential to Green politics can be found in Chapter 7 of John Barry's book *Rethinking Green Politics*.[5] Barry quotes, but then refutes the arguments of the 'terrible trio' of Ophuls, Hardin and Heilbroner, who saw some form of eco-authoritarian regime, with a scientific elite guiding decisions as necessary to deal with the scarcity inherent in the ecological crisis predicted by *Limits to Growth*. Although (unlike Barry) I share the fears of Ophuls *et al* as to the possible course of events in response to ecological constraints, for me there is a simple pragmatic reason for democracy. Without a consensus, an authoritarian regime would be subverted wholesale by two groups: a large, impoverished group, and a smaller, but more dangerous group who would be recognized as 'Bernards' from Chapter 2. To prevent this, the regime would have to become as repressive and ruthless as those in Nazi Germany, or in Iraq under Saddam Hussein. Such regimes have not normally been noted for consistency, but if the object of the exercise is a Green, sustainable economy, that too would be essential. So without a consensus, the consequences of trying to impose Green policies top down would be at best ineffective, and at worst frightful and probably still ineffective. Once a consensus, or at least a clear majority view in favour is accepted as essential to avoid these scenarios, then democracy makes far more sense as a means to implement it.

There is a body of opinion, which does not command a consensus, which maintains that reform of the money supply system is yet another precondition for a sustainable society. This complex topic must therefore be addressed, but rather than digress here at length, I have included it in Appendix II

(ii) Another look at some practical aspects

Up to now I have focused primarily on the medium and long term effects of introducing a Citizens' Income. However, technically, a Citizens' Income or an equivalent 'Tax Rebate' scheme could be announced by the Chancellor of the Exchequer in the Budget and be introduced in Great Britain within 12 months. The main obstacle to doing just that is of course that the public perception is as yet lacking. I have suggested that a CI is essential to Green politics, but the converse is also true. Once we achieve publicity, if we concentrate on publicizing the Citizens' Income (and localization) together with the connection with Green issues, so that everyone can visualise the effect on themselves in advance, their implementation need not be all that distant a prospect.

People on higher than average earnings will realize that they will be worse off, but as a proportion of their total income, most of them will be only marginally so. So their attitude is likely to depend on how close they are to the Green paradigm. For those largely in sympathy with Green ideas and not too far above the 'break even' point, a Citizens' Income twelve months hence might not seem the end of the world.[6] However, for higher incomes, there may well be a correlation between salary levels and hostility to the whole idea, especially the reasons for it. The twin aims of social justice and curbs on indiscriminate entrepreneurial activity will be equally infuriating. I doubt if the 'Bernards' I met whilst electioneering in 1974 will have shifted their ground very far. But if the situation is no worse than it was then (10% opposed to the whole idea), they ought not to be a bar to the electoral feasibility of an early implementation.

At the other end of the scale, the immediate effect on the unemployed will be nil. As I have explained, the CI opens up the potential for large numbers of additional low paid jobs, but very few will emerge on day one. Many people will have been working 'illegally' in the 'black' economy, and decriminalisation of what they are doing anyway may for them be neither here nor there. So we cannot necessarily assume that they will flock to support and bring about our new dawn. Other unemployed people will be suffering from varying degrees of demoralization and social exclusion, and again, they may not immediately recognize that the sea-change in prospect has anything to offer them. So we cannot rely on their gratitude either.

The immediate gainers in straightforward financial terms are of course those on low incomes – those now caught in the poverty trap. In Chapter 7 I quoted the example of a couple working at the minimum wage. Their net gain of £60 per week – a 36% increase- will be typical of many. Whilst the Citizens' Income does need to be implemented as soon and as quickly as possible, it may be that discontinuities on that scale suggest a more gradual phasing in than one year. But so far as a 'Greens using the media' scenario goes, at least this group ought to become our staunch supporters, even if they have never previously given the environment a thought. One opportunity which will be immediately apparent in many jobs is part time work sharing, which has not normally been an option for the principal earner in a two-parent family: time off in lieu of the full increase for a hard pressed carer, and an income top-up for someone else who was unemployed. It is unlikely that any other party will steal the policy from us, due to the large number of marginal losers, but the sooner the Citizens' Income is a topic of conversation, the sooner the subtle transition to Green attitudes postulated in Chapters 7 to 9 can begin.

However, there is a predictable difference of opinion which will crop up. Some will argue, with complete justification, that this large percentage increase in the incomes of the low paid does no more than correct a long standing injustice. Others will however point out the potential for helping businesses, including eco-friendly businesses, but also hard pressed businesses struggling either to export, or against cheap imports. As I have pointed out, what matters to an employee is total income, not whether it comes entirely from his employer. I would expect hostility from those concerned with social justice to the notion of using a Citizens' Income as a justification for lowering wage rates, but it is essential if the temporary commercial advantage postulated in Chapter 8 is ever to occur.

The principle that the relative levels of recruitment and loss could become the norm in wage negotiations, and it could favour either side. Once again, I base this prediction on the Siane strategy. The Citizens' Income brings about social justice, but potentially in the long term it also creates a genuinely free market, where the employee has equal bargaining power with the employer.[7] Any employer who tries to reduce wages will find that some workers begin to look for better offers, and he takes the risk that these will be the most competent. Such offers will be available due to the increased flexibility of the labour market generally, and the overall increase in low paid employment. Workers without high mortgage commitments will have basic needs covered without work. The 'correct' hourly rate will be that at which new workers willing to come and work at that rate are balanced by existing workers who are not.

One can certainly guess that there are some occupations where the hourly rate will rise, but Trade Union critics of the Citizens' Income envisage more hourly rates falling than rising. If hourly rates are indeed expected to fall overall, that could mean that introduction of the CI within twelve months of being announced is feasible after all, because the nominal cost to the better off would come down. But that would of course involve the simultaneous abolition of the minimum wage. As long as any of that massive increase for low paid workers due to the Citizens' Income remains, they are better off than they would be with a minimum wage.

There is a serious tactical problem in introducing a Citizens' Income in Britain over the question of housing costs. At one level, the CI is the implementation of a certain strategy – basic needs, but nothing else, to be provided from a communal fund. In practice it consists of shifting the main burden of paying for the prevention of poverty off the shoulders of those who narrowly fail to qualify for such help, and asking the better off to bear it instead. Anyone who has doubts about the CI must defend the existing stupid and unjust arrangements. There may be alternatives, but I have to say that of those of which I have heard during the past thirty years, none have come close. But the amounts involved in shifting this burden for the costs of accommodation are truly daunting. As has been mentioned already, in order to get over the novelty of the CI, it will have to be introduced at as low a level as possible. So at first accommodation costs will have to be dealt with nominally or not at all. But exactly the same principles apply as for any other basic need. Until accommodation can be placed on the same footing – an automatic sum to every individual sufficient to pay for a roof over her/his head – the claims made throughout this book as to flexibility, or bargaining power for workers as well as employers, will be severely restricted in scope.

(iii) Global considerations

We do not need to wait for the Citizens' Income, or whatever version of the Siane strategy is appropriate within each society to be actually adopted anywhere, for the same strategy to be thought about and applied as between nations. The need for an identity of interest when faced with ecological problems applies with even greater force at the global level. Third World countries are quite reasonably indignant at exhortations to care for their environment by more affluent nations. Just as the Citizens' Income is a right of citizenship, not a handout, so each nation should be entitled to a share of the earth's resources sufficient to cover the basic needs of its citizens. Debt relief would be an obvious first step. It may well be that for many communities, all that the Siane Strategy entails is to reinstate the wherewithal to provide their own necessities, for example allowing Ghanaian villages to grow their own rice as they used to, instead of forcing them to buy it from Thailand, at a profit to someone from a country richer than either. The globalizers claim that Ghanaian rice was 'inefficient', but that is according to their own narrow definition, serving their interests not those of the local people, who are in practice simply exploited as a market.

I have suggested earlier that population pressure might already be a factor in house prices and public attitudes in densely populated areas of Britain. This could therefore be a factor behind the hostility which has surfaced in some areas to asylum seekers. Of course there are more obvious factors such as insecurity and inadequate job opportunities, which the Citizens' Income should begin to address. From a human rights perspective, there should be no question of excluding people fleeing from oppression or worse. But these are often castigated as bogus on the grounds that they are merely 'economic migrants'. It is especially galling that implacable hostility is developing among the most deprived sections of British society, when it is globalization which is both widening the gap between rich and poor within nations, and aggravating the inexorable rise of economic migration, contrary to the promises made by the globalizers.[8] The true scandal, once the Siane strategy has been grasped, is that there is any pressure for economic migration in the first place. I shall return to the question of asylum seekers in the next Chapter.

There are major difficulties to contend with. Dislocations in local economies would have to be avoided by phasing in the new situation gradually and selectively. Where the Siane strategy does involve transfers of wealth between nations there would have to be some way of ensuring that it did indeed benefit all individuals, unlike much aid in the past. Is this possible without eroding the autonomy of governments even more than supra-national bodies such as the IMF have already done? On the other hand, I have pointed out in earlier Chapters that the Siane strategy does presuppose and even relies on aspirations above basic subsistence. Even before most of the world was distorted by colonial exploitation, the vast majority of people not in the top strata of their society have traditionally been accustomed to surviving on bare necessities or less. There must be a danger, especially in the Third World, that population might well simply increase without any relief of misery in the early stages. I say 'in the early stages', because I have sufficient confidence in Wilkinson's insight, quoted in Chapter 4, that any population in stable circumstances will eventually find an equilibrium at which all its members have a comfortable margin above mere survival. However, given the threats to the environment, not to mention the sheer scale of the population increase already, any aggravation is to be avoided, however temporary. Again, if it is accepted that freedom from fear of starvation is one prerequisite for reducing population growth, then a Citizens' Income, or whatever local adaptation of the Siane strategy is appropriate at the personal level, should be seen as one of the key solutions to this problem.

It seems particularly important that countries with rainforest should be encouraged to introduce some form of the Siane strategy internally as quickly as possible. The Tragedy of the Commons will ensure that transnational companies will continue to destroy rainforest as long as it remains profitable to do so. But at least the component of rainforest destruction that is due to sheer attempts to survive by poor people on its margins – at the expense of people content with their lot within the forest – could be rendered unnecessary fairly quickly.[9]

A particularly difficult application of the Siane principle concerns the former eastern bloc countries, especially the Russian Federation. But it is just as necessary. The former communist states had an appalling record of environmental abuse. Consequent on their economic collapse, and the behaviour of outside interests, particularly the globalizers, it is likely to get considerably worse, as even more appalling hunger and poverty becomes widespread. Already President Putin has cancelled a scheme intended to preserve the Siberian tiger from extinction, on the frank grounds that industrial regeneration takes priority. Irreplaceable Siberian tigers are a superficial concern compared to the ecologically destructive measures the Russian Federation may well deem necessary. The rest of the world cannot condemn any of this unless we offer some escape.

Escape of a sort is in prospect for some former communist bloc countries bordering on the EU. Five states, the Czech Republic, Hungary, Estonia Poland and Slovenia are in detailed negotiations to join the EU, and are already receiving assistance to meet environmental standards. However, as to the plight of others:

The danger is that they will ... become subject to the negative impact of European economic peripherality without the benefits. This would create the danger of locking them into a pattern of environmentally destructive economic growth and removing the incentive for improving environmental performance. The result would be a vicious circle of perpetual exclusion ... Even after the accession of the 'lucky five' there will be a need for continuing financial and policy assistance to ensure the integration of their unlucky brethren *(and the states of the former Soviet Union)* [my italics], into a 'common European environment.'[10]

However, even in the five states mentioned, the demands of growth and competitiveness in the global market outweigh any environmental help.[11]

The organized crime which is a consequence of the economic collapse, means that money which is desperately needed for the infrastructure – schools, hospitals, the police and so forth, is simply going into private pockets. Thus an urgent reason to alleviate the crisis in the former USSR is at the same time a serious aggravating factor militating against its implementation. There is no point in pouring resources into the Russian Federation and its immediate neighbours unless it does bring them back into Wilkinson's 'identity of interest in the face of ecological problems'. Yet again, we can see the outline of the Tragedy of the Commons. What way other than organized crime is there to protect oneself from the endemic deprivation? We can forget Garrett Hardin's 'mutual coercion, mutually agreed upon' as long as these mafias remain unaccountable, and the society on which they prey remains impoverished and desperate. Instead of the vision of a latter day 'Marshall Plan'[12] which was in the spirit of the Siane strategy, the collapse of the eastern bloc was seen as a 'get rich quick' opportunity by western businesses, an irresponsible blunder which will not be easy to repair. Can the Siane strategy at least help to bring about the international political will to heal these grievous wounds? As I said, it is not a panacea.

Notes and References

1   Such conflicts are of course expressions of the driving forces discussed in Chapter 3. As such, in the long term the Siane strategy will eventually have some relevance even here.

2   Hines, Colin (2000), *Localization – a Global Manifesto*, Earthscan, London.

3   Ponting, Clive (1991), *A Green History of the World*, Sinclair Stevenson, London.

4   In this context it is worth noting that the Working Families Tax Credit introduced by the Labour government in Britain in 1999 renders the single, and childless families at a disadvantage, and so operates as a population *increase* incentive.

5   Barry, J., *Rethinking Green Politics* (1999), Sage Publications, London; Ophuls, W., *Ecology and the Politics of Scarcity* (1977), Freeman, San Francisco; Hardin, G., *The Limits to Altruism* (1977), Indiana University Press, Indianapolis; Heilbroner R., *An Inquiry into the Human Prospect* (second edition 1980), Norton, New York.

6   I am personally in this category.

7   I have discussed in Chapter 7 (and do so again later in this chapter) the short term limitations on this flexibility, especially until accommodation can be included.

8   See Hines, Colin, *op cit,* especially Chapter 17, for a detailed account of the effect of globalization on developing nations.

9   Surprising progress is being made in Brazil towards the Citizens' Income principle. Several large cities have instituted Minimum Income Guarantee schemes, with some impact on the worst of the poverty. Unfortunately these tend not to apply in the more remote areas on the margins of the rainforest.

10 Quoted from Brian Slocock, 'Whatever happened to the Environment?' in Henderson, Karen (ed) (1999), *Back to Europe*, UCL Press, London, Chapter 9, p165.

11 Hines, Colin (2001), *From Seattle to Nice*. An unpublished paper for Caroline Lucas MEP.

12 The Marshall Plan was a system of massive economic aid by the USA to Europe for reconstruction at the end of the second world war.

XI

There are no Utopias either!

Some ideas on what a sustainable society might *really* be like

We do not have to return to the Siane way of life, only to adopt their basic strategy for sharing. However, anyone who has read *The Way* by Teddy Goldsmith will appreciate that there are other respects in which we need to emulate our pre-agricultural cousins. Gaviotas demostrates that high technology is not necessarily evil *per se*, but it will have to be brought under the control of the Gaian hierarchy which, as Goldsmith explains, guaranteed the stability and optimum functioning of life within the biosphere before the arrival of agricultural man.[1] As we saw in Chapter 1, although a balanced history of the world would explain that Gaia has always succeeded in reinstating equilibrium after numerous disruptions,[2] some sections of humanity have apparently outwitted Gaia for several millennia. Although this is brief in real terms, they have developed a formidable culture based on the assumption that they can continue to do so indefinitely.

Humans were not able to witness any of the previous occasions when Gaia re-imposed her will. I suspect that her methods were no more sensitive than for example the killing of sibling chicks by which some birds adjust their numbers to resources. Also since an aggressive strategy against one's own kind seems to confer an advantage as long as expansion is possible, during the closing stages of previous expansions following environmental disruption there must have been some ugly scenes as judged from a 'civilized' viewpoint. Yet Gaia demands only that we return to sustainability. There are ways of achieving this without tears, or at least with far fewer than are likely if we continue on our current path. We can keep the benefit of our technological expertise, indeed continued advances are quite feasible. We have the resources world wide to eradicate poverty, once there is an appropriate ethos, and those currently hindering this see a strategy which they can accept.

I believe that the politics of the foreseeable future will develop into tension and conflict between 'deep Greens' who will resist new developments on principle, and recent converts to sustainability who will pin their hopes on resource productivity.[3] Deep Greens will argue that no further disturbance of the biosphere is justified, and a steady state economy will be their ideal regardless of what else is feasible. Others will want to continue as close as ecological constraints allow to 'business as usual'. In the early stages the only realistic goal for Green politics will be to get high resource productivity and pollution control accepted as necessary – not merely desirable – preconditions for any further economic growth. However, even if that is the only change from current economic and political orthodoxy, what Greens have to offer, whether we or our listeners like it or not, must more closely resemble a recession by recent historical standards than would otherwise be the case, with the restricted choices that implies. Whether that is acceptable will depend on the paradigm individuals carry round in their heads.

At present it is taken for granted that economic growth is essential, on the grounds that a 'double-dip' recession is the inevitable consequence if it falters. The notion that the economic health of society depends on everyone consuming as much as possible, and in any case more than last year irrespective of what it consists of, or what its purpose is, seems incredibly fatuous in the light of the discussion in Chapters 4 and 5, and must be wrong if there is ever to be any hope of sustainability. But that does not mean that the conventional view can be dismissed out of hand. For example the Green ideal of goods lasting longer will have a real economic effect. Derek Wall describes the current Tragedy of the Commons driven dynamics as follows:

Even if we remove debt money, economic growth and artificial scarcity would still occur. If goods last longer firms make less profit but if we make goods that fall apart, if advertising is promoted to create new needs, firms will survive. Growth is necessary to create profit; a firm that lacks profit cannot invest in new technology and will be driven out of business by other companies that install new capital, so as to reduce costs. The crudest and most superficial reading of either orthodox or Marxian approaches suggests that, as production becomes more efficient, over-supply/a falling proportion of organic capital occurs so profits fall and the pressure is once again to grow so that they can be maintained. Schumpeter, in turn, outlines the process of creative destruction; a firm patents a new product and gains monopoly power, until the patent runs out, the firm is threatened and new research is fuelled. Survival occurs because firms research and develop new products, once again driving growth, The essential point to grasp is that in dealing with capitalism we are dealing with an evolutionary process. ... Capitalism, ... is by nature a form or method of economic change and not only never is but never can be stationary.[4]

In other words, it is impossible for Capitalism to aim for 'level flight'. If it is not going up, its descent cannot be controlled.[5] Depending on one's pre-Green ideology, the emphasis in the last sentence but one may be put on 'Capitalism' or on 'aim'. But the Siane demonstrate that sustainability at a comfortable standard of living does not preclude private enterprise, nor vice versa. Given the complexity of a developed economy, business failures are to be expected as more likely in a steady state than in an expanding one, but less likely than during the periods of recession which have been a persistent feature of growth.[6]

As long as there is a mechanism for recycling some of the money from the winners to the losers zero growth need cause neither undue hardship for the failures nor endanger the economy as a whole. I have compared the relative merits of Socialism and the Citizens' Income as such a mechanism, and argued in favour of the latter, because it allows entrepreneurial skill as much scope as possible. The bad news, as viewed by the winners under the present arrangements will be limited to the restrictions on their spending power implicit in higher levels of taxation than they have been used to. The Siane strategy will make it feasible, for the first time for several centuries, to aim for a steady state economy, that is where economic activity is neither expanding nor contracting. Quite apart from ecological limitations, aiming for permanent growth has always been unstable, and vulnerable to episodes of slump and deflation.

But is zero growth a necessary precondition for sustainability? I see no reason to discourage continued inventiveness. There will, or should be much scepticism and scrutiny of new ideas. Their proponents will be equally inventive in portraying them as ecologically sound, whatever their true merits. But every once in a while, new technology or practices will allow a period of time-limited economic expansion to take place. Certainly, starting from where we are there is much scope for economic activity which is not yet taking place, and which the Citizens' Income will facilitate: making existing buildings 'energy tight'; switching to organic farming; caring *properly* for the elderly, ensuring adequate resources for all public services (schools, hospitals, the Police etc.), and much more. It is even possible that a steady state economy may never be necessary. A continuous stream of *ecologically sound* innovations may allow economic growth as conventionally measured to continue seamlessly into the indefinite future. But we cannot be certain of that. We must demonstrate to ourselves that we can achieve and maintain a steady state economy whenever it *is* necessary. The ideal society will retain the ability to take advantage of new opportunities or technological innovations which are ecologically acceptable as and when they become available, but will otherwise be happy to settle for a steady-state economy, population size and life-style.

We know that the Siane (among many others) achieved a transition back from expansion to sustainability, if only because they live a long way from Africa, whence all our ancestors came. But we do not know whether the process was spontaneous or fraught and unwilling, as it is currently for the modern global community. Did they have to learn the hard way through the Tragedy of the Commons, or even a series of Tragedies?[7] However, it is possible that once the Citizens' Income is in operation, all that will be needed to effect economic 'take-off' or 'landing', at any rate in an advanced economy, will be to adjust the tax rates to go with it. For a steady state economy the Citizens' Income must be balanced by an equal amount in taxation. For expansion, tax rates could be cut, leading to a form of deficit financing.[8] When it is time to return to a steady state economy, the tax take can again be raised to equal the CI.

A sustainable society may take many different and unexpected forms and it would be rash to try to predict too many features. The Siane strategy is simply one of the most urgent and easily implemented. The strength of the Citizens' Income lies in the fact that it is the embodiment of a strategy which had been evolved to suit a sustainable lifestyle, which accepts the perceived limitations of the community's environment. The Siane were not living in Utopia prior to European interference. They had simply evolved ways of living indefinitely within their means, without internal conflict or hardship due to maldistribution. With our resources and technology we too can do the same, only more comfortably, but beyond that society will continue to be faced with all kinds of decisions and choices as it always has been.

One problem within a sustainable society which the Siane strategy cannot solve on its own is that individuals will need to feel they can identify a role for themselves. There is scope for all kinds of trouble if this need is not fulfilled, either spontaneously or by design. There is however quite a range of possibilities.[9] Many societies in ecological equilibrium were not averse to silly status games with whatever surplus they had over their needs as they defined them. Outrageous valuations on bizarre works of art could be a pointer in this direction. If nothing better emerges, that will at least be sustainable, and not too far removed from what happens now in the developed world.

One of the more sombre permanent problems is health – world health. Already the triumphalist cries of final victory over disease which were common at the height of economic expansion in the decades following the second world war have been muted. The ecological world view recognizes that this is a permanent war. From time to time a new disease will emerge, spread rapidly with the aid of modern means of travel, and like all its predecessors, eventually settle down as a long term unwelcome but manageable feature. There is scope for inhibiting and reducing the impact. Technology has for example been used successfully to contain Rabies. Used responsibly, instead of for profit, antibiotics could have held the inevitable at bay for considerably longer than now seems likely. But as with any other aspect of health care, and indeed life in general, this will involve difficult choices as to where to target finite resources.

Once the Siane strategy is accepted internationally, it should be axiomatic that no one need feel under pressure to migrate for economic reasons. When the huge task of implementing it is complete there should be no reason to hinder the movement of individuals between countries. When that stage has been reached, if there is a persistent pattern of large numbers trying to leave a country, then that ought to be valid grounds for the rest of the world to intervene, or at least to have an interest in the internal affairs of that country.

I have touched on the problem that the Green message will appear negative to anyone whose world view is still based on a belief that technology can underpin indefinite expansion. Whilst we Greens point to the mounting problems of congestion, resource exhaustion and pollution, those who retain their faith in expansion must always outbid us with promises to a still substantially consumerist society that we cannot match. Technological progress coupled with economic expansion has brought many undeniable benefits, as well as problems. Our message only becomes positive if you believe that the results will be better than attempts at expansion which fail. Nevertheless as Wilkinson has pointed out, all communities whose environment is stable find a *modus vivendi* in which all members are comfortable. Therefore once ecological constraints are accepted philosophically, life is potentially much more pleasant than promises of jam tomorrow which in practice mean a shortage of bread today for many.

Having spent the whole of this book so far advocating a Green paradigm, I must now qualify my case. The Siane had a wisdom which we ignore at our peril. I imagine nevertheless that their way of life has by now succumbed to outside influences. The brutal fact is that societies in harmony with their environment were no match for the onslaught of our own troubled society precisely because they had no problems which needed solving by developing their skills or technology. In fact, they are recognizable as unwitting 'Alfreds' in a Tragedy of the Commons.

Similarly, I have argued that whereas some aspects of our behaviour are uncomfortably mirrored in that of the chimpanzees, there is a more hopeful precedent set by our equally close relatives, the bonobos. But there are only 10,000 bonobos. Although chimpanzee populations are being decimated, there are still several million of them in the wild, from Tanzania to Senegal. If the chimpanzees ever managed to cross the River Congo into bonobo territory, they would probably exterminate the latter almost as fast as man seems likely to. The bonobos' non-aggressive ways are well suited to sustainability, but it is the chimpanzees who are better adapted to a competitive situation. So there are limits to the advantages of adapting single-mindedly to a sustainable way of life. We do need to preserve the ability to rise to challenges from outside.

It would be a misnomer to describe the society I envisage as ideal. It is simply a better option than the risks if we continue with our present attempts to prolong expansion, or the opposite, less immediate risks if (world) society does opt for permanent sustainability. It will be uncomfortable, or at least never settled. It must perform a perpetual balancing act between fostering conflict-resolution, and sharing attitudes and behaviour as the norm, without completely suppressing precisely those traits which will militate against these core values. At present competition backed by specious reasoning and thinly veiled, or sometimes naked aggression is driving the world towards destruction. Nevertheless we must resist the temptation, which may well become very strong, to try to outlaw competition and aggression completely. Gaia does permit these traits. She just sets clear limits to them.

An area that will be essential for the need to preserve otherwise unwelcome traits is of course sport. Its role may remain much as it is at present. Identification with the national or local football team is already a natural vehicle for much energy and enthusiasm, joy and despair. I should not be surprised if sport took on an even more prominent role in a society looking for alternatives to consumerism. Wherever possible, opportunities for competition within rules must be fostered, and even in an economy which denies itself indiscriminate expansion, this is an area which I would expect to repay generous investment handsomely. There will doubtless be many unforeseen ways in which people find satisfactory new aims in life. Provided they are sustainable, and do not infringe the rights or freedoms of others, they will be welcome.

Unfortunately it is I believe not coincidental that xenophobic hooliganism has also attached itself to the primary sport in Britain. Such behaviour is an instinctive expression of the underlying primeval drive to compete (for resources) by those whose only or most effective skill is violence. If only there were some way of allowing such groups to meet each other without troubling true sports fans, or indeed passers-by with children who want nothing to do with them, it might prove to be a necessary safety-valve. Straightforward prevention and deterrence of such behaviour are obviously essential, but it may prove too widespread and recurring a problem simply to suppress it.

I fear that the need to channel rather than to suppress aggression will be a prevalent problem among many human populations. Given the millennia during which our ancestors have pursued an expansionist strategy more or less continuously, the instinct to keep on going for expansion, and the aggressive, competitive approach which goes with it will die hard. Moreover, it seems reasonable to suppose that those who have a 'gut' feeling that this is the right strategy will tend to have selectively emigrated to the new world. In that case areas colonized by Europeans (not those remaining in Europe) may be more prone to attempts to continue or restart expansion, though there were other pressures leading to emigration.

I believe that Japan might reveal some useful clues. A strand of Wilkinson's thesis was in effect 'necessity is the mother of invention'. However, in the course of the inventions born of necessity, Western Europeans inevitably became technologically superior to all the cultures they encountered in the course of their expansion, even the Chinese, who had originally had a head start. The newcomers dominated all the societies they met with one outstanding exception – Japan. Having lived in a state of apparently unchanging stability, stagnation even, for several centuries, they suddenly took on the West as equals. How were they able to do this? Why did Japan, and only Japan take to western technology and the competitive ethos like a duck to water?

All too often Japan has joined the USA in the role of 'Bernard' in the ecological play 'The Tragedy of the Commons'. But could they just as effortlessly return to a state of unchanging traditions? I shall now make an extremely rash prediction. Assuming the Citizens' Income does enter the mainstream debate in the not too distant future, I would advise Great Britain not to dally too long before introducing it. If they do, I believe Japan will, not for the first time, capitalize on a western invention. Their economy has been ailing for several years. I would expect them to use the temporary competitive edge possibly offered by the Citizens' Income quite ruthlessly as long as competition remains the name of the game. However, when the time comes to call a halt by international agreement, I predict that Japan will be the nation which has the least difficulty in making the transition.

I have suggested in earlier chapters that although those coming from a 'social justice' perspective initially assimilate more easily as Greens, the Siane strategy will allow certain attitudes commonly identified as 'right wing' to make more sense than hitherto. I have already dealt with 'free market' aspects, but the Siane strategy validates ideas on personal responsibility for one's actions in exactly the same way. At present it is still fair comment to claim that much antisocial behaviour is generated or aggravated by the injustices and inequalities in society. As society becomes more inclusive and cohesive, there will be more reason to hold individuals responsible for their actions. Individual responsibility will of course be particularly important on the question of stabilizing population. However, these aspects will not impinge until well into the future.

Throughout this book I have somewhat loosely referred to a 'space capsule Earth', or a 'sustainability' world view. Perhaps I ought now to clarify the difference between them. Ultimately there may be periods, possibly quite long periods, during which quite strict ecological rules will have to be observed. The penalties for offending against these rules have been demonstrated by the Easter Islanders. These rules will cover resource use, pollution, population size, and any other aspect of human activity which impinges on sustainability. Agonizing choices will have to be made on matters of health care for example. Such rules may have to be enforced quite soon if current trends in exploitation continue. The effect of the exponential principle is that the exhaustion point not only comes sooner than was expected, it can also come quite suddenly, as the Grand Banks fishermen, the Easter Islanders and the Maya civilization all found out to their cost.

However, if we can persuade ourselves – globally – to renounce maximum exploitation before we actually have to, we can allow ourselves to be much more relaxed about population size, use of non-renewable resources and other constraints whilst developing alternatives. Although we must never forget those photographs of the Earth looking like a little capsule in Space, 'sustainability' can be defined much less strictly. If the breathing space before we do finally have to be strict with ourselves can be extended from decades to centuries, it will not seem nearly as painful. In fact it need not be painful at all.

In a way, the colonization and exploitation of the rest of the world by Europeans flowed naturally from the hierarchical structure which causes the underlying pressure. Instead of as hitherto in history and pre-history going back to our ape forbears, a dominant group simply pushing others aside, and if necessary engaging in attrition until only one group survived, how much more advantageous it was to take over a group along with their wealth as a resource, just like the lower orders in one's own society. In the light of this, the current attitude of Western entrepreneurs to both the third world and the collapsed communist regimes, though despicable, is merely a natural extension.

Many Greens suspect that there is a conspiracy maintaining the *status quo*. But what does such a conspiracy consist of? I have suggested that 80% of the population are still unimpressed or actually hostile to Green ideas, down from 90% thirty years ago. If one assumes only proportions at least as high among the media and those in positions of power, and then factors in the pressures of the Tragedy of the Commons on any with misgivings and the declared aims and confrontational approach of some anti-global-izers, then the degree of suppression of subversive ideas observed is much as is to be expected.

But it is simply not in anyone's interests to continue as we are. No one, however rich and powerful, is safe from the effects if pressures to wreak ecological damage continue. Under the Siane strategy, the elites will lose marginally, but if they are clever enough they can remain relatively rich and powerful. They may even remain relatively rich and powerful indefi-nitely. But they will have added bonuses. They will no longer need to fortify their homes They will no longer risk being shot during a business trip to Moscow. We have already seen that internally, the plundering approach to the economic opportunities in the former Soviet bloc has been a factor in the rise of formidable organized crime there.

The Siane strategy offers those in control a much more palatable alter-native to the complete dismantling of their power which has hitherto been the only apparent option canvassed. Moreover, the rationalizations for business as usual, and the invitation to developing nations to 'take advan-tage' of free trade will increasingly be revealed as bogus once the Siane

Strategy has become a world-wide paradigm. Whatever they have to pay out as a Citizens' Income or Foreign Support (not aid) will give entrepreneurs extremely good value for money. The more rainforest, fertile river valleys or other parts of the biosphere that can be restored, not merely preserved, the more wealth there will be for them to compete over – and on a permanent basis.

Notes and References

1   Goldsmith, Edward (1996), *The Way*, Themis Books, Dartington.
2   Ponting, Clive (1991), *A Green History of the World*, Sinclair Stevenson, London.
3   Resource productivity is discussed in the Introduction.
4   Wall, Derek (2002), *A Critique of Social Credit*, unpublished ms, quoting Schumpeter, Joseph Alois (1976), *Capitalism, Socialism and Democracy*, Allen and Unwin, London p.82.
5   Whilst he is not advocating zero *growth*, of relevance here is Samuel Brittan's suggestions on zero inflation: '...I once nearly made a permanent enemy of Stanley Fischer, before he became Deputy Manager of the IMF, by suggesting a long term aim of price stability instead of a never-ending series of inflation targets... Of course any move towards zero inflation should be taken very gradually with plenty of time to look listen and learn ... 'The required short-term flexibility would be provided by accepting greater year to year fluctuations in the price level than are tolerated under present inflation target regimes.' From Samuel Brittan, 'Alternatives to inflation targets', *Financial Times* 01/03/01.
6   There are alternatives to Schumpeter's theories about growth and depressions. Profits may not be a reward for innovation (Schumpeter), but a deduction from the value created by labour (Marx) or a reward for the abstinence of capitalists (Mill). (From Heilbroner, Robert L. (1986), *The Worldly Philosophers*, sixth edition, Penguin Books, 1991.) Explanations for economic depressions include theories about profit rates (Mandel), prices (Rostow), social structure (David Gordon), and investment (Forrester), as well as the theory about innovations (Schumpeter).
7   According to a BBC2 *Horizon* programme broadcast on 9 January 2003, by the time of the first visit by Europeans in 1722 little more than a century after the crisis described in Chapter 2, the surviving

inhabitants of Easter Island appeared to have a settled, if impoverished way of life.

8   In 1972 Sir Keith Joseph, a member of Mrs. Thatcher's Conservative
    cabinet, produced a Tax Credit Scheme which amounted to a
    Citizens' Income in the form of a Tax Credit. It was *not* to be backed
    by taxation, with the express purpose of stimulating economic
    growth.

9   A discussion of personal goals in a Green society can be found in
    Chapter 7 of Toke, Dave, *Green Politics and Neo-Liberalism* (2000),
    Macmillan Press, London.

XII

Summary and conclusion

In the early chapters of this book I contrast the responses to ecological limits of two human societies untouched by Western influences: Rapanui (Easter Island) and the Siane. The world as a whole is arguably on the same course as Rapanui, the lunacy being driven by exactly the same forces. The Siane demonstrate that such a disastrous outcome is not inevitable. The essential difference between them is that on Rapanui it was their first attempt. The Siane had had several millennia in which to evolve a *modus vivendi* which was satisfactory both to themselves and to Gaia.

Chapters 6 onwards outline a series of possible steps by which we might yet escape the fate of Rapanui and take advantage of the Siane strategy. I have admitted that they are conjectural, and none are inevitable:

1   The establishment of the Citizens' Income somewhere, as the form appropriate to an advanced Western country of the only strategy on which prosperous sustainability has ever been based by any human group, namely the provision of basic necessities from a communal fund;

2   That country using it to slightly reduce consumption internally, whilst retaining the ability to supply the rest of the world's unabated demands;

3   This having the potential to confer a slight commercial advantage on that country;

4   (All) other developed countries adopting the CI to neutralize that advantage;

5   This facilitating a shift towards a 'sustainability' paradigm by millions of individuals within the developed world;

6   The emergence of a powerful Green political movement based on this paradigm;

7   The re-alignment of politics with sustainability versus expansion as the major division;

8   Recognition that the Siane Strategy is just as valid and vital between

nations as between individuals, and must be implemented world-wide;

9   The new paradigm achieving a near consensus world-wide; which will make possible:

10   Genuine restraint among those who are currently profiting from destroying the biosphere, and effective control of the minority who will continue to do so regardless.

These steps can be further summarised by answering the question 'How do we stop the Tragedy of the Commons running its full course?', This must include the proposition that a world-wide alternative consensus is needed. Such a consensus can be based on a strategy which on the one hand guarantees freedom from want without the need for economic expansion, and yet allows wealth creators (who currently include those who pose the gravest threat) maximum scope within the rules necessary to safeguard the biosphere.

Even if you dismiss the whole of the foregoing reasoning, I must reiterate one basic fact. The Citizens' Income is the provision of basic necessities for all from a common fund. That fund will be provided by members of the community as a whole according to ability to pay. This will replace the present system whereby basic necessities for those below the poverty line are paid for by those only just above it. If you do not understand the last sentence, please read Chapters 6 and 7 again. This is a principle as fundamental as Marxism seemed 150 years ago. That ideology was adopted by several nation states. Indeed, the Siane strategy, of which the Citizens' Income is an expression, is arguably as close as Marxism to the dictum 'From each according to his ability, to each according to his needs'. This alone validates the CI in the Green context even if it has none of the far reaching consequences I claim for it. However, without the ecological connection, as long as a neo-liberal paradigm is dominant, there appear to be numerically more losers than gainers. This is a chicken and egg problem. One of the claims I do make for the Siane strategy is that it can and must challenge the neo-liberal paradigm.

As long as there is uncontrolled expansion of either population or economic activity, the Tragedy of the Commons is in motion. And until the Siane strategy forms the basis of a world wide consensus, none of the major players in the frightening game of world poker which is triggered by the Tragedy dare be the first to pull out. The escape plan set out here may seem improbable, but it is possible. The same logic applied to both the slave trade and the use of child labour. The first to renounce either risked putting themselves at a commercial disadvantage, but an overwhelming consensus nevertheless developed in each case, and they did disappear. Before dismissing the thesis outlined here, please bear in mind that Gaia will re-establish a sustainable regime sooner or later. We may – or may not – live to regret not devising our own methods instead of leaving it to her default settings.

I said at the beginning that this book sets out a series of inter-related ideas which have been buzzing around my head for years. To tell the truth, I am tired of trying and failing to get them across piecemeal in 'sound bites'. It is only when taken as a whole, and especially when linked to localization, that they develop what for me is a powerful logic. But just as Marxism became a force to be reckoned with *before* it was adopted anywhere, the Siane strategy and localization can become the focus of a new world movement *now*. It need not entail any of the unpleasantness which accompanied Marxism in practice, and it is more relevant to the situation we now face.

My own dream, which sits oddly with the purpose of this book, is of space travel, and I would not even rule out colonization. Once we have mastered the art of not ruining ecosystems wherever we go, once we have achieved a state of not having to go to new places or bring in innovations just because there is a pressing economic need, once we have learnt how to 'land' the economy as easily as 'take-off', and sharing basic needs is automatic, world wide, then space exploration could be a legitimate use of resources. Just as I have no problem with astronomical salaries or wealth provided no one is going short and the environment is protected, I see nothing wrong with the 'extravagance' of astronomical exploration. I am not an expansionist by nature, but I am insatiably curious about the rest of the Universe. Indeed, if we are serious about permanent sustain-ability for the human race, then insurance in the form of colonies beyond the Earth might seem no more than prudent, given the rare, but real threat from asteroid or comet strikes. If I were a young person growing up in a society looking for alternatives to consumerism, that would probably be mine.

Postscript

A t first sight the terrorist attacks on the World Trade Center in New York on 11th September 2001 have no immediate connection with the proposals set out in this book. The motives of the alleged instigators, Osama Bin Laden, and the al-Qa'ida network have nothing to do with either sustainability or globalization. Their stated complaints against the USA are confined to matters relating to Islamic countries, and are otherwise unrelated to economic injustices which could be laid at the American door. These injustices may have been among the motives of the perpetrators, but those identified appear to have come from affluent backgrounds.

However, I believe that there is a very real connection with the problems outlined. I have argued that we humans are balanced on a cusp where it is touch and go as to which of two very different primal strategies we choose to deal with environmental problems, xenophobia or some form of conflict resolution. The Siane strategy and localization can offer an alternative to the dominant 'neo-liberal' globalization paradigm, but there is already a challenger in the field: religious fundamentalism. Xenophobia triggers behaviour which can temporarily relieve the pressures caused by failing to live within environmental constraints. I believe that both the aggressive attitude of the USA government and the motives of Islamic extremists stem from this all too natural human response.

The immediate precipitating causes of wars often mask underlying ecological pressures. That Osama bin Laden is one of 54 siblings has been mentioned as an irrelevant curiosity. I am not so sure. Any society not in ecological equilibrium will be prone to the Tragedy of the Commons. This includes all societies of European descent, and all Islamic nations. If both continue to expand, mutual hostility or worse is inevitable. The less dramatic primal programme based on conflict resolution may be adopted if sustainability can become a reality in time. If not, then the instinct to slip into a war mentality is never far below the surface.

The ethos of the United States ever since it emerged as a world power has been one of exploitation of resources and people. Prior to the World Trade Center outrage, the new administration of George W. Bush had taken this attitude to extremes with a series of decisions trampling on international agreements, not least the Kyoto Protocol on climate change. It is therefore not surprising that the USA had greater difficulty than it should in obtaining universal condemnation and isolation of its attackers. Its conduct and attitude since that attack has been increasingly combative, and seems likely to produce like-minded enemies. Yet in the longer term, some good may emerge. Several commentators have made the point that from now on the USA can neither retreat into isolationism nor continue to ride roughshod over the rest of the world in pursuit of its own unbridled interests. Under a President with the humility to accept this advice, and to try conflict resolution in place of force, it would not be a huge step to an acceptance of the Siane strategy.

Appendix 1

An attempt to assess the core level of support for the Green Party nationally at the general election on 7th June 2001, and to compare this with previous performance

Of the total of 145 constituencies contested by the Green Party, I have identified 53 'paper' candidates. These fall into three groups: 15 'safe' Conservative seats, plus one Liberal Democrat; 12 safe Labour seats; and 25 where the result was likely to be perceived by the voters as being in doubt. The definition of this was that the constituency changed hands, or the majority was less than 2,000 in either 1997 or 2001. I have however included two other constituencies, Llanelli and Yeovil, where the swings were significantly greater than the average.

In the 'safe' seats, I have tried to apply a fairly strict definition of 'paper candidate': a 'Freepost ' leaflet; not more than 5,000 additional leaflets; minimal street activity (local activists to decide); no meetings arranged by the Party attended by more than 25 persons not known to the organizers; no publicly arranged meetings attended by significant numbers of undecided voters (which would be unusual nowadays); no local councillors, or local results better than 10%; no significant TV coverage, and no press coverage more often than once per week.

In the marginals, I have relaxed this definition. The rationale is that there are two sets of circumstances where the Green Party's core level of support nationally can be derived: a) where the result depends effectively on the Party's national profile only, but where the likely outcome in that constituency is not at issue; and b) where the value of local efforts is likely to be 'squeezed' due to the result being in doubt. These are also the constituencies where the bigger parties can be assumed to have targeted resources. I have identified five constituencies, Boston & Skegness, Carshalton & Wallington, Eastleigh, Kingston & Surbiton and Norwich North where the tactical squeeze was likely to be so severe that any local GP activity would be irrelevant. These constituencies are especially valuable in identifying core Green support where voters may have perceived the choice of government to be at stake.

The average Green poll in the 53 constituencies was 1.91%. This breaks down into 2.12% in the safe conservative seats, 1.95% in the Labour seats, and 1.76% in the marginals. To put this in context, in the two 1974 elections, 10 PEOPLE (i.e Green Party) candidates in comparable circumstances[1] polled 0.8% on average. In 1979 this rose to 1.43%, when local activity was still non-existent. It fell to 1.38% in 1997, even though by then there were local factors boosting results in some areas. However, bearing in mind the level of apathy, in order to make a more accurate comparison with the past, I have added a final column, giving the 2001 percentage as if the total turnout had been 75%.[2] Against this criterion the overall average is 1.54%, the (safe) conservative average 1.76%, Labour (where apathy was greatest) 1.44%, and in the marginals 1.46%. The average in the 5 'squeezed' constituencies was 1.29% actual, or 1.01% 'corrected'. The comparison here is with by-election results such as Walsall North, 1975 (0.5%) or Newbury 1993, (0.59%).[3]

Finally, I have tried to assess the effect, if any of competition from other small parties, but this does not appear to be significant.

Notes

1   I have excluded constituencies where a Green Party candidate was not opposed by a Liberal or Liberal Democrat candidate. This has not happened since 1974. In that year, in Coventry North West for example, a PEOPLE candidate polled over 1,200 votes, or 3.5%. Whilst this was a useful comparison with the relative success of the Values Party in New Zealand in 1972, where there were only two major parties, it would have given a false impression if included in this comparison.

2   The comparison with a 75% turnout is based on the assumption that the small numbers seriously considering voting Green in a parliamentary election are less likely than others to share in the general apathy. A possible contrary argument (for which I am indebted to Alison Marshall) is that random votes would be more likely to favour small parties.

3   'Squeezed' constituencies are similar to by-elections in that any Green Party activity is rendered ineffective by the resources poured in by the three major parties

4   In the final column of the results table, swings greater than 6% are in bold type, on the grounds that a greater degree of uncertainty is likely to reduce the effectiveness of any Green efforts.

Green Party 'paper' candidates in the 2001 General Election (See pp134-135 for definitions. For abbreviations see p142).

	Green vote 2001	Green %	1997 Maj	2001 Maj	% Poll 01 cf 75%	Other small parties	Swing[4]
Aldershot	630	1.39	Con 6621	Con 6564	57.9	1.07	UKIP Ind Loony	1.13
Ashford	1353	2.82	Con 5355	Con 7359	62.5	2.35	UKIP	2.84
Ashton-u-Lyne	748	2.09	Lab 22965	Lab 15518	49.11	1.36	BNP	2.59
Banbury	1281	2.49	Con 4737	Con 5219	61.77	2.05	UKIP	1.02
Batley & Spen	595	1.54	Lab 6141 Gain	Lab 5064	60.54	1.24	UKIP	0.03
Beckenham	961	2.11	Con 4953	Con 4959	63.07	1.77	UKIP Lib	0.89
Bishop Auckland	1052	2.73	Lab 21064	Lab 13926	57.23	2.08		4.85
Bognor Regis & Littlehampton	782	2.01	Con 7321	Con 5643	58.25	1.56	UKIP	0.64
Bolton NE	629	1.61	Lab 12669	Lab 8422	56.03	1.20	Soc Lab	2.06
Boston & Skegness	521	1.29	Con 647	Con 515	58.42	1.00	UKIP	0.06
Bradford N	611	1.74	Lab 12770	Lab 8969	52.69	1.22	BNP	2.44
Calder Valley	1034	2.18	Lab 6255 Gain	Lab 3094	62.98	1.83	UKIP Cannabis	2.27
Cardiff C	661	1.9	Lab/LD 7923	Lab/LD 659	58.28	1.47	PC Soc All UKIP	**8.43**
Carshalton & Wallington	614	1.51	LD/Con 2267 Gain	LD/Con 4547	60.31	1.21	UKIP	3.26
Chelmsford W	837	1.74	Con 6691	Con 6261	61.49	1.42	UKIP Cannabis	0.62
Cheltenham	735	1.76	LD/Con 6645	LD/Con 5255	61.92	1.45	Loony UKIP	0.32
Dewsbury	560	1.53	Lab 8323	Lab 7449	58.79	1.19	BNP UKIP	0.5
Eastleigh	636	1.34	LD/Con 754 Gain	LD 3058	63.77	1.07	UKIP	2.54
Ellesmere Port & Neston	809	1.95	Lab 16036	Lab 10861	60.94	1.58	UKIP	2.18
Faversham & Mid Kent	799	1.95	Con 4173	Con 4183	60.37	1.56	UKIP Loony	0.89
Gower	607	1.63	Lab 13007	Lab 7395	63.37	1.37	Soc Lab PC	5.11
Hastings & Rye	721	1.75	Lab 2560 Gain	Lab 4306	58.36	1.36	UKIP Ind Loony	2.62
Henley	1147	2.58	Con 11167	Con 8458	64.27	2.21	UKIP	1.31
Isle of Wight	1279	2.01	LD/Con 6406 Gain	Con 2826 Gain	59.72	1.60	UKIP Ind IOW SL	**6.61**
Kingston & Surbiton	572	1.17	LD/Con 56 Gain	LD 15676	67.54	1.05	UKIP Soc Lab	**15.92**
Llanelli	515	1.42	Lab/PC 16039	Lab 6403	62.25	1.17	PC Soc Lab	**10.62**
Ludlow	871	2.02	Con/LD 5909	LD 1630 Gain	68.39	1.84	UKIP	**8.27**

	Green vote 2001	Green %	1997 Maj	2001 Maj	% Poll 01 cf 75%	Other small parties	Swing[4]
Luton S	798	2.03	Lab 11319 Gain	Lab 10133	57.04	1.54	UKIP Soc All	1.13
Milton Keynes SW	957	2.17	Lab 10292 Gain	Lab 6978	59.24	1.71	UKIP Cannab SA	2.45
Newcastle/Tyne E & Wallsend	651	1.99	Lab 23811	Lab 14223	53.17	1.41	Soc Lab Comm	8.53
Norfolk N	649	1.15	Con 1293	LD 483 Gain	70.22	1.07	UKIP	1.53
Norfolk S	1069	1.91	Con 7378	Con 6893	67.62	1.72	UKIP	0.22
Norwich N	797	1.75	Lab 9470 Gain	Lab 5863	60.89	1.42	UKIP Ind 211	2.17
Redditch	651	1.76	Lab 6125 Gain	Lab 2484	59.21	1.38	UKIP	3.49
Rochdale	728	1.85	Lab/LD 4545 Gain	Lab 5655	56.7	1.39	Ind 253	2.45
Rotherham	577	1.97	Lab 21469	Lab 13077	50.67	1.33	UKIP Soc All	**6.24**
Ruislip Northwood	724	1.95	Con 7794	Con 7537	61.1	1.58	BNP	1.46
Runnymede & Weybridge	1238	2.92	Con 9875	Con 8360	58.14	2.26	UKIP	0.27
Rutland & Melton	817	1.74	Con 8836	Con 8612	64.95	1.50	UKIP	0.76
Selby	902	1.79	Lab 3836 Gain	Lab 2138	64.51	1.53	UKIP	1.28
Shrewsbury & Atcham	931	1.87	Lab 1670 Gain	Lab 3579	66.58	1.66	UKIP Ind 258	2.08
Stratford/Avon	1156	2.11	Con 14106	Con 11802	64.42	1.81	UKIP	0.61
Swansea E	463	1.54	Lab 25589	Lab/PC 16148	52.51	1.07	PC UKIP	**9.15**
Swansea W	626	1.95	Lab 14459	Lab 9550	56.24	1.46	PC UKIP Soc All	2.99
Tiverton & Honiton	1030	1.85	Con 1653	Con 6284	69.17	1.70	UKIP Lib	4.23
Wakefield	1075	2.61	Lab 14604	Lab 7954	54.46	1.89	UKIP Soc Lab Soc All	4.82
Wansdyke	958	1.95	Lab 4799 Gain	Lab 5113	69.35	1.80	UKIP	0.83
Wantage	1062	2.16	Con 6039	Con 5600	64.53	1.85	UKIP	0.31
Watford	900	1.94	Lab 5792 Gain	Lab 5555	61.24	1.58	UKIP Soc All	0.75
Waveney	983	2.08	Lab 12453 Gain	Lab 8553	61.59	1.70	UKIP Soc All	1.93
Witney	1100	2.24	Con 7028 Gain	Con 7973	65.93	1.96	Ind UKIP	1.87
Wolverhampton SW	805	1.97	Lab 5118 Gain	Lab 3487	60.88	1.59	UKIP	0.97
Yeovil	786	1.63	LD11403	LD 3928	63.35	1.37	UKIP Lib	6.47
53 Averages		**1.90**			**60.82**	**1.54**		**3.00**

Safe Conservative or Liberal Democrat

	Green vote 2001	Green %	1997 Majority	2001 Maj	% Poll	cf 75%	Other small parties
Aldershot	630	1.39	Con 6621	Con 6564	57.9	1.07	UKIP Ind Loony
Ashford	1353	2.82	Con 5355	Con 7359	62.5	2.35	UKIP
Banbury	1281	2.49	Con 4737	Con 5219	61.77	2.05	UKIP
Beckenham	961	2.11	Con 4953	Con 4959	63.07	1.77	UKIP Lib
Bognor Regis & Littlehampton	782	2.01	Con 7321	Con 5643	58.25	1.56	UKIP
Chelmsford W	837	1.74	Con 6691	Con 6261	61.49	1.42	UKIP Cannabis
Cheltenham	735	1.76	LD/Con 6645	LD/Con 5255	61.92	1.45	Loony UKIP
Faversham & Mid Kent	799	1.95	Con 4173	Con 4183	60.37	1.56	UKIP Loony
Henley	1147	2.58	Con 11167	Con 8458	64.27	2.21	UKIP
Norfolk S	1069	1.91	Con 7378	Con 6893	67.62	1.72	UKIP
Ruislip Northwood	724	1.95	Con 7794	Con 7537	61.10	1.58	BNP
Runnymede & Weybridge	1238	2.92	Con 9875	Con 8360	58.14	2.26	UKIP
Rutland & Melton	817	1.74	Con 8836	Con 8612	64.95	1.50	UKIP
Stratford/Avon	1156	2.11	Con 14106	Con 11802	64.42	1.81	UKIP
Wantage	1062	2.16	Con 6039	Con 5600	64.53	1.85	UKIP
Witney	1100	2.24	Con 7028 Gain	Con 7973	65.93	1.96	Ind UKIP
16 **Averages**		**2.11**			**62.38**	**1.76**	

Safe Labour

	Green vote 2001	Green %	1997 Majority	2001 Maj	% Poll	cf 75%	Other small parties
Ashton-u-Lyne	748	2.09	Lab 22965	Lab 15518	49.11	1.36	BNP
Bishop Auckland	1052	2.73	Lab 21064	Lab 13926	57.23	2.08	
Bolton NE	629	1.61	Lab 12669	Lab 8422	56.03	1.20	Soc Lab
Bradford N	611	1.74	Lab 12770	Lab 8969	52.69	1.22	BNP
Dewsbury	560	1.53	Lab 8323	Lab 7449	58.79	1.19	BNP UKIP
Ellesmere Port & Neston	809	1.95	Lab 16036	Lab 10861	60.94	1.58	UKIP
Gower	607	1.63	Lab 13007	Lab 7395	63.37	1.37	Soc Lab PC

	Green vote 2001	Green %	1997 Majority	2001 Maj	% Poll	cf 75%	Other small parties
Newcastle/Tyne E & Wallsend	651	1.99	Lab 23811	Lab 14223	53.17	1.41	Soc Lab Comm
Rotherham	577	1.97	Lab 21469	Lab 13077	50.67	1.33	UKIP Soc All
Swansea E	463	1.54	Lab 25589	Lab/PC 16148	52.51	1.07	PC UKIP
Swansea W	626	1.95	Lab 14459	Lab 9550	56.24	1.46	PC UKIP Soc All
Wakefield	1075	2.61	Lab 14604	Lab 7954	54.46	1.89	UKIP Soc Lab Soc All
12 Averages		**1.94**			**55.43**	**1.43**	

Result in doubt

	Green vote 2001	Green %	1997 Majority	2001 Maj	% Poll	cf 75%	Other small parties
Batley & Spen	595	1.54	Lab 6141 Gain	Lab 5064	60.54	1.24	UKIP
Boston & Skegness	521	1.29	Con 647	Con 515	58.42	1.00	UKIP
Calder Valley	1034	2.18	Lab 6255 Gain	Lab 3094	62.98	1.83	UKIP Cannabis
Cardiff C	661	1.9	Lab/LD 7923	Lab/LD 659	58.28	1.47	PC Soc All UKIP
Carshalton & Wallington	614	1.51	LD/Con 2267 Gain	LD/Con 4547	60.31	1.21	UKIP
Eastleigh	636	1.34	LD/Con 754 Gain	LD 3058	63.77	1.04	UKIP
Hastings & Rye	721	1.75	Lab 2560 Gain	Lab 4306	58.36	1.36	UKIP Loony 338
Isle of Wight	1279	2.01	LD/Con 6406 Gain	Con 2826 Gain	59.72	1.60	UKIP Ind IOW SL
Kingston & Surbiton	572	1.17	LD/Con 56 Gain	LD 15676	67.54	1.05	UKIP Soc Lab
Llanelli	515	1.42	Lab/PC 16039	Lab 6403	62.25	1.17	PC Soc Lab
Ludlow	871	2.02	Con/LD 5909	LD 1630 Gain	68.39	1.84	UKIP
Luton S	798	2.03	Lab 11319 Gain	Lab 10133	57.04	1.54	UKIP Soc All
Milton Keynes SW	957	2.17	Lab 10292 Gain	Lab 6978	59.24	1.71	UKIP Cannab SA
Norfolk N	649	1.15	Con 1293	LD 483 Gain	70.22	1.07	UKIP
Norwich N	797	1.75	Lab 9470 Gain	Lab 5863	60.89	1.42	UKIP Ind 211
Redditch	651	1.76	Lab 6125 Gain	Lab 2484	59.21	1.38	UKIP
Rochdale	728	1.85	Lab/LD 4545 Gain	Lab 5655	56.70	1.39	Ind 253
Selby	902	1.79	Lab 3836 Gain	Lab 2138	64.51	1.53	UKIP
Shrewsbury & Atcham	931	1.87	Lab 1670 Gain	Lab 3579	66.58	1.66	UKIP Ind 258

1.53

	Green vote 2001	Green %	1997 Majority	2001 Majority	% Poll	cf 75%	Other small parties
Tiverton & Honiton	1030	1.85	Con 1653	Con 6284	69.17	1.70	UKIP Lib
Wansdyke	958	1.95	Lab 4799 Gain	Lab 5113	69.35	1.80	UKIP
Watford	900	1.94	Lab 5792 Gain	Lab 5555	61.24	1.58	UKIP Soc All
Waveney	983	2.08	Lab 12453 Gain	Lab 8553	61.59	1.70	UKIP Soc All
Wolverhampton SW	805	1.97	Lab 5118 Gain	Lab 3487	60.88	1.59	UKIP
Yeovil	786	1.63	LD11403	LD 3928	63.35	1.37	UKIP Lib
25 Averages		**1.75**			**62.42**	**1.45**	

Result in doubt (UKIP only other small party standing)

	Green vote 2001	Green %	1997 Majority	2001 Majority	% Poll	cf 75%	Other small parties
Batley & Spen	595	1.54	Lab 6141 Gain	Lab 5064	60.54	1.24	UKIP
Boston & Skegness	521	1.29	Con 647	Con 515	58.42	1.00	UKIP
Carshalton & Wallington	614	1.51	LD/Con 2267 Gain	LD/Con 4547	60.31	1.21	UKIP
Eastleigh	636	1.34	LD/Con 754 Gain	LD 3058	63.77	1.04	UKIP
Hastings & Rye	721	1.75	Lab 2560 Gain	Lab 4306	58.36	1.36	UKIP Loony 338
Ludlow	871	2.02	Con 5909	LD 1630 Gain	68.39	1.84	UKIP
Norfolk N	649	1.15	Con 1293	LD 483 Gain	70.22	1.07	UKIP
Norwich N	797	1.75	Lab 9470 Gain	Lab 5863	60.89	1.42	UKIP Ind 211
Reddich	651	1.76	Lab 6125 Gain	Lab 2484	59.21	1.38	UKIP
Selby	902	1.79	Lab 3836 Gain	Lab 2138	64.51	1.53	UKIP
Shrewsbury & Atcham	931	1.87	Lab 1670 Gain	Lab 3579	66.58	1.66	UKIP Ind 258
Wansdyke	958	1.95	Lab 4799 Gain	Lab 5113	69.35	1.80	UKIP
Wolverhampton SW	805	1.97	Lab 5118 Gain	Lab 3487	60.88	1.59	UKIP
13 Averages		**1.66**			**63.18**	**1.39**	

Result in doubt (other small parties: Soc All Soc Lab but not UKIP)

None

Result in doubt (other small parties: UKIP Soc All Soc Lab Lib)

	Green vote 2001	%	1997 Majority	2001 Maj	% Poll	cf 75%	Other small parties
Kingston & Surbiton	572	1.17	LD/Con 56 Gain	LD 15676	67.54	1.05	UKIP Soc Lab
Luton S	798	2.03	Lab 11319 Gain	Lab 10133	57.04	1.54	UKIP Soc All
Watford	900	1.94	Lab 5792 Gain	Lab 5555	61.24	1.58	UKIP Soc All
Waveney	983	2.08	Lab 12453 Gain	Lab 8553	61.59	1.70	UKIP Soc All
Yeovil	786	1.63	LD11403	LD 3928	63.35	1.37	UKIP Lib
5 Averages		1.77			62.15	1.45	

All constituencies where BNP also stood

	Green vote 2001	Green %	1997 Majority	2001 Maj	% Poll	cf 75%	Other small parties
Ashton-u-Lyne	748	2.09	Lab 22965	Lab 15518	49.11	1.36	BNP
Bradford N	611	1.74	Lab 12770	Lab 8969	52.69	1.22	BNP
Dewsbury	560	1.53	Lab 8323	Lab 7449	58.79	1.19	BNP UKIP
Ruislip Northwood	724	1.95	Con 7794	Con 7537	61.1	1.58	BNP
4 Averages		1.82			55.42	1.34	

BNP only other minor party

	Green vote 2001	Green %	1997 Majority	2001 Maj	% Poll	cf 75%	Other small parties
Ashton-u-Lyne	748	2.09	Lab 22965	Lab 15518	49.11	1.36	BNP
Bradford N	611	1.74	Lab 12770	Lab 8969	52.69	1.22	BNP
Ruislip Northwood	724	1.95	Con 7794	Con 7537	61.1	1.58	BNP
3 Averages		1.92			54.3	1.39	

Severe squeeze

	Green vote 2001	Green %	1997 Majority	2001 Maj	% Poll	cf 75%	Other small parties
Boston & Skegness	521	1.29	Con 647	Con 515	58.42	1.00	UKIP
Carshalton & Wallington	614	1.51	LD/Con 2267 Gain	LD/Con 4547	60.31	1.21	UKIP
Eastleigh	636	1.34	LD/Con 754 Gain	LD 3058	63.77	1.13	UKIP
Kingston & Surbiton	572	1.17	LD/Con 56 Gain	LD 15676	67.54	1.05	UKIP Soc Lab
Norfolk N	649	1.15	Con 1293	LD 483 Gn	70.22	1.07	UKIP
5 Averages		**1.29**			**64.05**	**1.09**	

For comparison, the results in previous by-elections where a 'severe squeeze' operated were as follows

		Green vote	Green %
4.11.75	Walsall N	150	0.5
1984	Bermondsey	90	0.3
6.5.93	Newbury	341	0.59

Abbreviations:

BNP	British National Party
Comm	Communist
Con	Conservative
Lab	Labour
LD	Liberal Democrat
PC	Plaid Cymru
Soc All	Socialist Alliance
Soc Lab	Socialist Labour
UKIP	United Kingdom Independence Party

Appendix 2

Monetary reform:
Two contrasting views within the Green Movement

Chapter 10 explored what other preconditions there might be for a sustainable society in addition to a satisfactory sharing strategy. On most topics a degree of consensus among Greens can be derived from the subject matter, but that is not the case so far as the money supply is concerned, so this requires special consideration. Those in favour of reform argue that this is another *sine qua non*. There are several statements of the case for monetary reform available,[1] but its proponents also include many who do not share a Green world view.[2]

Briefly the case for reform within the Green context is that the present system causes a mismatch between the money supply and society's needs; it results in a cycle of booms and slumps; it gives the banks the power to decide who gets to use money and why, society's needs being irrelevant; it results in growing indebtedness; and high levels of interest widen the divide between wealth and poverty. Crucially, the growth in the money stock means that either the economy must grow (regardless of ecological considerations) or there must be price inflation, though both can of course occur at the same time. The proposed remedy is the removal of money based on interest-bearing debt and its replacement by money spent into circulation by the government, which would not be a debt, but simply a medium of exchange. Banks would be limited to lending the amount they have on deposit or reserve.

The arguments appear cogent to a layman, though a large body of Green Party members remain perplexed. Reform is supported by some formidable authorities, including for example the New Economics Foundation. Furthermore, Greens are inevitably at odds with conventional thinking in other areas so that it feels intuitively right that yet another radical reform may well be essential, or that the banks, as agents of the capitalist system, may be at the root of the problem. I am however one of a number of sceptics. Jonathan Dixon, an accountant by profession, points out certain technical flaws in the case for reform, and he argues that the money supply system is neutral, and hence irrelevant to the furtherance of Green ideals. He demonstrates that interest can be legitimate as the reward of deferred use, though both sides agree that there are circumstances, notably third world debt, where lending at interest is abused.

Dixon points out that although money once consisted mainly of coins made of precious metal with an intrinsic value, all that is really needed is a medium of exchange. Provided confidence is maintained, much more economic activity can be financed by treating bank deposits in the same way as if they were gold coins. The key to money creation over and above tokens valuable in themselves (or treated as if they were) lies in its 'double entry' nature: for every debit there is a credit somewhere, and vice versa. At first sight the absence of 'reserve requirements' whereby banks must not lend beyond a given ratio to the gold or deposits in their reserves seems irresponsible from the standpoint of Green economics. Greens are keenly aware of the need to limit economic activity to the resources available. But *that* is what business dealings ought to be limited in relation to, not an arbitrary reference point, such as a quantity of gold or the amount of money already on deposit.

I take the view that the arguments put forward for reform are describing *symptoms* rather than causes. In Chapters 4 and 5 I drew attention to the fact that humans, at least most of them, have been out of ecological balance for at least 10,000 years. The last 250 have seen an unprecedented acceleration of this imbalance. I have argued that this imbalance will inevitably continue until either a crisis occurs analogous to that on Easter Island, where there were no banks, or a sharing strategy consistent with sustainability is adopted. As long as pressure for economic growth exists, it will require a monetary mechanism. An initially cumbersome and restrictive monetary system has been streamlined into one which facilitates maximum economic growth with ruthless efficiency, apart of course from the breakdowns due to the instability inherent in expansion.

But does the monetary system actually *compel* growth? Is there a vicious circle? That the problems monetary reform addresses are symptoms does not rule them out as causes. Borrowers include all businesses engaged in competition with each other, so that these arguably have no option but to borrow if they are not to drop out of the rat race. Compulsion to borrow may be irrelevant as long as there is an overwhelming consensus in favour of economic growth, but this pressure may hamper a change in actual behaviour by a participant not sharing that consensus. However, it is arguably the competition which creates the pressure, the monetary system being merely a mechanism.

There is an important category not under any compulsion either by competition or the monetary system: consumers, among whom it is the aggregate of people's expectations – the expansionist ethos – which is at the root of the problem. Some borrowing is due to maldistribution under a faulty sharing strategy, but some is consumer driven, by the high expectations which might be realistic in an economy which does have room for expansion. It is the would-be borrower who clamours for a loan for a new business venture which he is sure will be a money-spinner, for a £300,000 house or to buy a new car when interest rates are low, or to fit a new kitchen every time he moves. Once the Siane strategy, and the ecological world view it makes feasible for individuals has started to percolate into people's consciousness, it will at least be possible for the inflammation on the body politic to subside naturally. When/if it does, the money supply will, on this reading, fall into line with it without reform.

'Debt free' money spent into circulation by the government, and intended to be a permanently circulating medium of exchange may be feasible. In fact there are historical examples, notably the 'Greenbacks' issued during the American Civil War. But that does not establish that it is necessary even now, let alone in the still unexplored circumstances of a consensus in favour of a steady state economy. I have suggested in Chapter 11 that in a steady state economy a Citizens' Income would be balanced by taxation, whereas during periods when growth could be justified as consistent with sustainability, the CI would be paid, but not matched in full by taxation. This would be 'money creation' as per the reform proposals, and yet quite consistent with Dixon's view. The difference is reduced to one of semantics: according to Dixon, this is the government going into debt, whatever 'spin' you put on it. However, Dixon also points out that cash is technically a debt owed by the Bank of England which can be ignored provided it stays in circulation permanently. The same may apply to a debt incurred to finance the CI.

Until a strategy is adopted which will allow millions of individuals to contemplate zero economic growth with equanimity growth will remain essential, and any notion of giving priority to Green principles must be secondary. I have discussed in Chapter 11 whether and to what extent zero economic growth may occur. Suffice it to say for this discussion that a Green society would be well advised to plan for it as an option. But as long as there remains a body of consumers still unsympathetic to the Green world view the proposed reforms would simply infuriate them.

However, when that message has begun to be accepted, it may be that restrictions on the availability of private credit would be appropriate, and would be accepted as part of a holistic Green package. If monetary reform is indeed a sound proposition, then and only then some form of it may quite possibly be adopted naturally.

Despite the polarization of this debate, there is common ground. Both sides are agreed that usury – debt entered into under duress – is unacceptable. This applies to national debts incurred by Third World countries just as much as to individuals. All deplore the secrecy and inaccessible lending criteria currently exercised by the banking system. Banks wield too much power, and greatly encourage the creation of money by aggressive marketing of loan facilities. Neither side disputes that the banks do this without adequate consideration of the sustainability of the undertaking being financed.

Monetary reform has proved to be an abstruse topic, not really understood by many who have tried. Getting the Siane principle accepted will be difficult enough without any avoidable burdens. If, as some of us consider, the arguments are inconclusive, the scientific principle of 'Occam's Razor' dictates that we should try the hypothesis with the fewest assumptions first. If it ain't broke, don't fix it.

References

1   Rowbotham, Mike (1998), *The Grip of Death*, Jon Carpenter Publishing, Charlbury.
    Douthwaite, Richard (1999), *The Ecology of Money,* Green Books, Dartington.
    Leslie, Brian, 'The Fallacies of Monetary Reform', *Sustainable Economics* Vol. 7 No 2 March 1999. Obtainable from 12 Queens Road, Tunbridge Wells, TN4 9LU.
2   Early Day Motion 1515, tabled before parliament by Austin Mitchell MP on 26 June 2002, included 'high economic growth' among the objectives of debt free money.

Bibliography

Axelrod, Robert (1984) *The Evolution of Co-operation*, Basic Books, New York, Penguin Books, London

Barry, John (1999) *Rethinking Green Politics* , Sage Publications, London

Beaumont, Tim (1997), *The End of the Yellow Brick Road*, Jon Carpenter, Oxford

Brittan, Samuel (1995), *Capitalism with a Human Face*, Edward Elgar, Cheltenham

Cann, Rebecca L., Stoneking, Mark & Wilson, Allan C. 'Mitochondrial DNA and Human Evolution,' *Nature,* 325 (1987), pp31-6

Daly, Herman (1973), *Toward a Steady State Economy*, Freeman, San Fransisco

Descola, Philippe (1993), *Les Lances du crépuscule* Librairie Plon; English translation (1996) *The Spears of Twilight* Harper Collins, London

Douthwaite, Richard (1999), *The Ecology of Money*, Green Books, Dartington

Firth, Raymond (1936), *We, the Tikopia*, Stanford University Press.

Goldsmith, Edward (1996), *The Way* Themis Books, Dartington

Goodall, Jane (1986), *The Chimpanzees of Gombe*, Harvard University Press, Cambridge Mass.

Hardin, G. (1968), 'The Tragedy of the Commons', *Science* 168

Hardin, G. (1977), *The Limits to Altruism*, Indiana University Press, Indianapolis

Heilbroner R. (1980), *An Inquiry into the Human Prospect*, Norton, New York (second edition)

Heilbroner R. (1986), *The Worldly Philosophers*, Penguin Books, London, (sixth edition 1991)

Slocock, Brian, 'Whatever happened to the Environment?' in Henderson, Karen (ed) (1999), *Back to Europe*, UCL Press, London, Chapter 9

Hines Colin (2000), *Localization – A Global Manifesto*, Earthscan, London

Lambert, Jean (1996), *No Change? No Chance*, Jon Carpenter, Oxford

Lomborg, Bjørn (2001), *The Skeptical Environmentalist*, Cambridge University Press, Cambridge

Meadows, D., Randers, J. and Behrens, W. (1972), *Limits to Growth*, Universe, New York

Ophuls, W. (1977), *Ecology and the Politics of Scarcity*, Freeman, San Francisco

Ponting, Clive (1991), *A Green History of the World*, Sinclair Stevenson, London

Rowbotham, Michael (1998), *The Grip of Death*, Jon Carpenter, Charlbury

Schumacher, E. F. (1973), *Small is Beautiful: Economics as If People Really Mattered*, Abacus, London

Toke, Dave, (2000), *Green Politics and Neo-Liberalism*, Macmillan Press, London

Van Parijs, Philippe (1995), *Real Freedom for All*, Oxford University Press

de Waal, Frans B.M., 'Bonobo Sex and Society', *Scientific American*, March 1995, pp82-88

Wall, Derek (2002), *A Critique of Social Credit*, unpublished ms

Wilkinson, Richard (1973), *Poverty and Progress*, Methuen, London

Internet references

Gaviotas & Easter Island
'The 2020 Challenge, by Duane Elgin. 6. Two Scenarios: An evolutionary crash and bounce.' www.newhorizons.org/future/elgin2020f.html
The author has tried without success to contact Duane Elgin for permission to reproduce his text.

Grand Banks Fisheries
'Cod don't vote. How politics destroyed Atlantic Canada's fisheries'
ElisabethBrubaker@nextcity.com or Perspective@nextcity.com

Index

tax credits 57, 68, 121 (note 8)
taxation, 57-69, 71-72, 76, 78, 83,
 111, 120, 121, 145; airport landing
 tax 99, 102; disguised tax 60-62, 78;
 land 68; resource tax 68, 97
Thatcher, Mrs. 65, 79, 92
trade unions 73, 78, 81-82, 89, 90
Tragedy of the Commons 9, 10, 17-
 29, 31, 38, 40, 46, 48 (note 8), 52,
 53, 83, 91, 93, 96-104, 108, 109,
 115, 116, 119, 121, 123, 124, 126,
 130, 132, 144

unemployment 71-72, 74-75, 78-79,
 89, 90
unemployment benefit 73
United Nations Conference on the
 Human Environment, Stockholm,
 1972 6
United States 52-53, 93, 124, 132-133

Value Added Tax (VAT) 68

Values Party 101
van Parijs, Philippe 80 (note 7)
Verts, Les 85
Voynet, Dominique 85

Waal, Frans B. M. de 37-38, 53
wage rates 71-73
Wall, Derek 119-20
Way, The 118
Wilkinson, Richard G. 46-48, 115,
 122
Worcester, Tracy, Marchioness of 88
work, casual 71-72; work ethic 78-81;
 part-time work 71-72
Working Families Tax Credit
 (WFTC) 62, 64, 72, 109 (note 4)
World Bank 28
World Trade Center 132
World Trade Organization (WTO) 28

xenophobia 31-40, 123, 132